TO LAUR

ALWAYS SPEAK
YOUR TRUTH

Joy Jennings.

I'M NOT YOUR "BABY"

An Australian Woman's
Tortured Life of
Sexual Harassment and Assault

A memoir

Joy Jennings

In recounting the events in this memoir, chronologies have been compressed or altered to assist the narrative. Where dialogue appears, the intention was to recreate the essence of conversations rather than verbatim quotes. The names and identifying details of the characters in this book have been changed.

I'm Not Your "Baby":
An Australian Woman's tortured life of sexual harassment and assault

Print Edition
ISBN 978-0-9940962-0-3

Cover photo by D.L. Neuf
Published by AJP Publications
Printed by Createspace

First Edition 1234567891

Author's Note

Names have been changed as have other identifying factors in selected cases, and some dialogue has been recreated, but otherwise the stories and characters in *I'm Not Your "Baby"* are true.

Acknowledgments

It is with deep gratitude that I thank my life partner. Without his loving encouragement, his belief in the truth and care for me as a human being, my story would not have made its rightful journey into the world. Thank you, for you have lived part of this story.

Chapter 1

I could hear him quite clearly through the bedroom window and more than likely, the neighbours could as well. "Come on. Do something, will ya!" he barked. His impatience wasn't helping, I was already feeling completely ridiculous and didn't need to be bullied.

Sitting stiffly on the edge of his bed, I tried to grasp what he wanted me to do exactly. He dashed outside to take up his spectator's position so quickly that I wasn't even given the chance to respond to his proposition of giving him "a show." I had never done anything even remotely erotic before. I was only nineteen for goodness sake, and he didn't even wait for me to respond. If I *had been* given a choice, I would have said no without hesitation. I was too young, too inexperienced and far too embarrassed to do such a thing at my awkward age, but now he was out there waiting and expecting to be sexually entertained.

The pressure was intensifying and so was my heart rate. I felt forced into doing at least *something* before he became too upset. I reached into my handbag, which I'd dropped on the floor just forty minutes earlier, and retrieved my hairbrush. Slowly and nervously, I began stroking my hair. My jittering had to have been obvious. I'd hoped he could see from my shaking hand and strained face, just how incredibly foolish I was feeling, and maybe he would drop the whole thing, but he didn't seem notice or care.

"Yeah that's it, good! Now go over to the dresser and look at yourself in the mirror," he instructed. "No don't look at me, I want you to pretend that you don't know I'm out here watching you," he ordered.

I did what I was told and moved reluctantly over to the stool in front of the dresser, barely glancing at my reflection.

"Okay, now I want you to start undoing the buttons on your shirt and, as you do, look at yourself and get all turned on, okay?" he directed. The arousal in his voice didn't turn me on at all. Rather, it was making me really quite annoyed. I didn't like being forced into doing something I wasn't comfortable with, especially by someone who was supposed to care for me.

"I don't really want to do this Mikey," I called out as I turned to face him standing outside, begging him with my eyes.

"Oh, come on. Don't be such a baby. What's the big deal?" he snapped.

I sighed from the defeat and could see I had no choice but to continue. I turned back around and fixed my eyes on my shirt, touching my fingers to the last button. I fumbled with it, giving the impression it was difficult to unfasten, stalling for more time while trying to formulate some escape plan. I couldn't think of one damn thing.

When I finally *managed* to undo it, I glanced back at the window. He was eagerly leaning in and waving at me to continue. I hesitated, drawing in a rutted breath as if about to do battle with the devil himself. Then, while exhaling, I unbuttoned the middle and top two buttons in quick succession. My white, cotton shirt was now loose and open at the front.

"Good," he praised. "Now move the shirt aside and start playing with your tits." My body instantly flooded with a searing heat. It felt like a burning combination of pressure, intense fear, hate and anger.

"Mikey, I don't want to do this," I called out, hoping he would take my objection seriously. I just wanted him to come back inside and treat me the way I needed him to, like a real girlfriend. I needed tenderness and affection, not to be put on show like some porn star or stripper inside a glass booth.

"Oh, come on. Why won't you do this for me?" he continued.

His reaction was not only disappointing, but I was also unprepared with an answer. All I could offer him was a shrug from my shoulders while holding back tears that were now pooling in my eyes. I had finally reached breaking point.

Rising from the stool, I made my way over to the bed and lifted up his comforter. In one swift movement, I slid down underneath it, covering myself in an awkward shame. I just wanted his ridiculous sex game to be over and no longer cared if he was going to be upset.

It was at that moment I felt completely overcome by a whirlwind of fragmented and horrible memories. Dozens of them, all swirling around me at once. Every one of those memories carried the same feelings of burning pressure, fear, anger and hate. My past, for the first time that it presented itself in this way, was now having a profound effect on an essential part of me, and it was going to be impossible to explain to Mikey. I couldn't even really explain it to myself. Whatever was happening, it was filling me with such anxiety that it rendered me powerless to do anything. I became emotionally, physically and sexually paralysed.

Am I permanently damaged already? Or is this just acute shyness that is simply a normal reaction at my age? My mind started reeling in confusion. *Why on earth would he expect me to be turned on by being watched from outside the window? That just creeps me out beyond belief!* My only boyfriend prior to Mikey had never asked me to *perform* for him, so this was all new to me. Besides, I had only been dating him a few months, so I wasn't even sure if I liked him enough yet to participate in these fantasies of his.

I hadn't noticed that he had returned inside, and was now standing before me, shaking his head with disapproving eyes, annoyed that I'd ruined his fantasy. He was expecting an explanation.

"I just don't like being watched, Mikey, and I feel like a complete idiot doing that stuff. I'm sorry." I was hoping that would be enough. I wanted nothing more than a reassuring hug and an apology. *If he wants that stuff, then he needs to go somewhere and pay for it.*

"Well you should grow up and stop being so frigid." He remained cross. Not the reaction I was hoping for. The next ten minutes we spent in a verbal tennis match without any resolve. I thought it was probably best just to go home.

I climbed out from the bed, re-buttoned my shirt and gathered my things, hoping he would stop me from leaving. He didn't, so I faced a thirty-minute walk home by myself.

* * *

Walking the streets of Australia's Gold Coast, especially at night, wasn't the best option for a girl by herself, but my car was out of service, I couldn't afford a taxi and there wasn't a bus for another hour. My only choice was to go it alone.

I avoided the main highway and took the side roads, striding the pavement briskly with my head down in serious determination. I had taught myself to do that to try to circumvent the harassment I usually encountered.

My thoughts sprinted off ahead of me. *What if Mikey is some sick kind of pervert, the type that gets off while peering in at unsuspecting girls through their windows?* I started to feel ill from the thought but then became stricken with a spasm of guilt. Maybe I overreacted. Perhaps he had simply lifted a shade on a window I didn't know was there, and I now had to try to make sense of a screwed up, intricate connection between my past and my present. Was it unfair to expect my boyfriend to know what my sexual limitations were when I didn't know myself? But then again, what if he *was* some kind of pervert going around the neighbourhood looking in windows? *That's a messed up thing to do!*

I was jolted out of my thoughts by a blasting horn from a carload of young blokes. They whistled and called out at me as they drove past, and I really wasn't in the mood for it.

"Woohoo! Hey, baby, bend over for us, will ya? We're horny!" they yelled.

Although I was used to it, even by the tender age of

nineteen, their vile remarks always had the same perturbing impact on me every time. They drove away, hooting, hollering and tooting. Street harassment was part of my life whether I liked it or not.

I dashed the final hundred metres home, feeling reduced to nothing but a cheap sex object by every male that I had encountered that evening.

* * *

Nervous about waking my parents, I slipped into bed as quietly as a cheating husband would. As I lay tossing and turning, too full of the night to sleep, I felt myself being dragged into a dark tunnel of ugly memories. Although I didn't want to face the torment of what lay within it, the tug was too strong.

I was suddenly back in my bedroom of my old house in Melbourne where we grew up. The year was 1980. I was fourteen, and it was a time in my life when my neighbour had been watching me from outside my bedroom window.

The first time I saw him looking in at me, I was changing by my wardrobe. For some reason, perhaps it was God or The Universe—to me it's the same thing only with different names—I felt a quiet nudge to look out my window. It felt like a whisper within my gut, alerting me of something.

I looked out and could see an eye peering at me through a small hole in our fence that separated our properties. I immediately scrambled to cover myself with my clothes, scurrying behind my closet door. My heart leapt, initially from fright and then confusion, as my adolescent brain tried to process my new awareness.

Who was that? Was that my neighbour? Why was he looking at me? Didn't he know I was half naked? Why didn't he turn away? Aren't people supposed to look away if they see you undressing? Doesn't he realize I'm just a kid? I felt not only confused but also annoyed that I was suddenly and so rudely stripped of my privacy, and I felt way too embarrassed to move, although I knew I had to. Terrified of being seen, even though I had managed to cover myself back up, I decided to crawl "combat style" across the floor and out the door to safety. I don't know why I didn't tell my parents, but I just went outside, found my siblings and hung around close to them as they entertained their friends.

That wasn't even close to the end of it. I saw that eye many more times. Its unremitting surveillance had become a constant menace, and over time I had become quite terrorized by it. I sensed a male was behind it. No woman, I believed, would gaze in at a girl in that way. What confused me the most was that I wasn't sure if what he was doing was actually wrong. *Do adults have the right to look in at me whenever they like? Is this wrong, or is he simply checking in on me to make sure I am okay? Should I tell someone, or will I be scoffed at if I do?*

Deep within my core, frequent whispers warned me of wrongdoing, but because I was taught to always obey adults, I disregarded my gut and gave credence to my earlier teachings. That led me to tolerate him watching me. Never once did I report his watchful eye to anyone, assuming adults had rights I didn't know about.

This continued for about a year, until his perverted activities finally ended one evening when he overshot his confidence and became way too cocky.

My entire family was out, apart from my father who was watching television in the living room. Less than a minute after entering my bedroom, I heard a noise outside my window. I looked over and saw a shadowy male figure framed within it. A face, blackened by the night, was staring in at me only an inch from the glass. It frightened me tremendously.

I don't know why I didn't scream. Perhaps it was the shock, or maybe I was so used to having an audience that I had become numb over time. He didn't move at all. It was at that moment I felt a real threat of danger, so I gingerly slipped out of my room in the attempt to fetch Dad without letting him on.

Despite being the one who should have been panicking, I had to remain composed so I could deal with my father's response. My dad, despite being a good-fun daddy 40% of the time, the other 60% was a liquor-loving, hot-headed sonofabitch, and this was going to surely set him off.

"Now please don't get mad, but there is someone outside my bedroom window," I stated as softly as I could, flinching for his unavoidable overreaction.

Without hesitation, he immediately rose and hollered, "Who? Who is out there?"

My stomach twisted and my knees buckled, leaving me incapable of anything more than a frightened shrug. He dashed out of the room, bolted through the kitchen and out into the laundry to fetch his flashlight. That thing was so large and heavy it could not only light up a night sky but also beat the crap out of someone if necessary. With his "weapon" in hand, he bolted to the front door, kicked it open with his foot and positioned himself on the front step. "Who's out there?" he shouted.

Two seconds later, a blur of a man ran out from the side of the house in one swift motion. He scampered over our front lawn, leapt through our pampas grass bush, which would have surely sliced his skin, and darted out onto the street. He bolted like an athlete in a fifty-metre dash up the footpath in a desperate attempt to savour his last few moments of freedom. Dad gave chase and sprinted after him. He ran as fast as he could. Then, about halfway up the street, Dad stopped abruptly. He lifted his flashlight and pointed it directly at the perpetrator, catching him in the beam of light.

"I've got you, Peter. I've got you now. You might as well give up, Peter. I have you," Dad called. *Peter? Who the heck is Peter?* I then put two and two together. *That has to be someone familiar if he knows his name. It has to be him, the eye from next door!* The man stopped dead in his tracks, slumped his head and shoulders, slowly turned around and began slinking back.

Dad maintained his rigid position on the footpath and waited until this man returned to him, like a drill sergeant expectant that his commands would be followed to the letter. Once he surrendered himself, my father grabbed the back of his shirt and marched him back to our property. He shoved him down the two front steps, pushed him hard along our garden path then slammed him up against the brick wall beside the front door.

It all felt so surreal. My heart pounded wildly. It was almost like watching a scene from one of Dad's TV cop shows, but this was real!

He then proceeded to beat this guy over the head with his flashlight, shouting and calling him all sorts of names I shouldn't have heard at that age. He was practically unleashing his full wrath on this guy. I wasn't sure what I was more shocked about, watching my daddy beating someone up or hearing him swear!

"Go inside and call the police Midget, quick!" Dad commanded with urgency. Midget was my family pet name and one that put me in my place as the smallest and youngest of four children.

In the time it took for me to run inside, dial the number, explain the situation, answer a couple of questions and be told the officers were on the way, Dad had forced our perpetrator inside and thrust him down into one of our lounge chairs in the living room.

Dad furiously paced back and forth along the living room carpet, breathing so heavily that I thought he was either going to have a heart attack or kill this guy with his bare hands. The man he wanted to kill was sitting anxiously on the edge of the chair, leaning forward, resting his head in his hands and his elbows on his knees, which were shaking uncontrollably. He shook his head continually and kept repeating, "I wish I was dead. I wish I was dead. Oh God, I wish I was dead."

Curiously, the man didn't appear anything like I had imagined him. The entire time he had been watching me through the fence, I thought the eye belonged to someone much older, perhaps in his sixties or seventies. I imagined him with a scruffy, more weathered appearance, like one of those dirty perverts on Dad's TV cop shows. But he was unlike that in every way. Although I still hadn't seen his face thoroughly, from his clothes, his shoulder-length hair and youthful, although panicked voice, he would have been no older than mid-thirties. His average, unassuming appearance would have caused no alarm to anyone, being someone you would say hello to without a moment's hesitation.

My thoughts were interrupted by the police arriving at the door, and no sooner had I let them in, than I was sent off to my room. I wasn't happy about it. In fact, I was pissed off that I didn't get to see that pervert being cuffed and taken away. I stayed in my room as I was told but tried intently to listen to the muffled voices through my door. I couldn't make out clearly what they were saying.

After half an hour or so, I heard the rest of my family returning home, and a few minutes after that, my mother entered my room. She sat down on my bed and asked me if I was okay.

"Yeah, I guess." I shrugged.

She gave me a loving kiss on my forehead and settled me under the blankets without discussing anything about what had happened. I assumed Dad had filled her in.

With crazy adrenalin still pumping through my veins, I found it impossible to sleep, lying wide-eyed and too hyped to settle.

What seemed like forty minutes later, I heard a car pull up outside the house next door. A minute later, female voices began getting louder in my neighbour's kitchen. One of them escalated into a high-pitched squeal. "He's where? What the hell?" This was followed by banging and crashing sounds. The same car that had arrived only a few minutes earlier screeched off up the road. Then, the neighbourhood was silent.

I was never told what happened to my neighbour and the matter was never discussed again after that night. It was all swept under the carpet, and the once or twice that I brought it up, mostly from natural curiosity, the subject was quickly averted without explanation. I assumed I was not supposed to ask any more questions, so I never did.

It taught me that things of that nature were to be just forgotten about. It seemed that if we didn't talk about horrible things, then they would all just dissolve somewhere in the back of our minds never to worry us again. It wasn't quite that simple.

The memory of that entire year of being watched by a stranger, and its dramatic conclusion, remained with me forever. That man robbed me of not just my privacy but also my innocence and trust. I lost a part of who I was and what I believed about the world, especially about adults.

None of what I went though was going to translate well with Mikey though. He wasn't the type who would understand what it meant to have that experience at such a delicate age. He was led by his libido and only interested in playing out his sexual fantasies and getting off. He couldn't possibly understand what was going on inside me.

As I lay in my bed, slowly emerging from my tunnel, I thought it was probably best if Mikey and I spent a couple of days apart. I needed to spend some time with my girlfriends anyway. *I think I'll call my friend Tina in the next few days and see what she's doing. Maybe we can go shopping, or to lunch, or to the beach.*

Chapter 2

On the way to meet my friend Tina at the main beach in Surfer's Paradise a few days later, I had to walk by the dreaded Birdwatchers Bar on the main corner. It was the busiest pub in town, made popular by men who loved to watch "birds" walk by.

Every manner of beer swillin', red-blooded Aussie bloke lined up day and night for that prime position right beside the large open windows. They could not only perv on all the chicks, but hurl catcalls, taunts and whistles at them as they walked past. I had been subjected to their onslaughts many times before. As I began to approach, I stiffened and held my breath in anticipation of the inevitable.

"Hey, baby, that's a fine ass you got there!" one sung out.

I ignored him. *Wanker*.

"Oh, babe, don't do it to me! You'd better walk fast, because you're teasing me beyond my control!" another one remarked.

Is that guy actually warning me that he cannot control himself, and I'm going to be sexually attacked? That doesn't make me feel very safe. Why should my safety be compromised just for walking along the street? I quickly dashed by, annoyed and fearful, looking back over my shoulder as I scurried off in the direction of the beach. *Dirty old perverts*.

Tina was already at our designated spot, sitting on a towel, and she waved me over. I took a small comfort in knowing I now had a friend to protect me if needed. She was sitting with a couple of male friends, something I wasn't expecting. She introduced me to them.

"G'day, how's it goin'?" they greeted in typical Aussie bloke fashion.

I smiled and nodded.

"We're goin' in for a dip. Youse comin'?"

"Not just yet. Joy and I are going to catch up for a bit,"

Tina replied, shielding her eyes from the sun.

"Suit yourselves." They shrugged and raced each other towards the water.

Lying on our towels, basking in the warmth, we gossiped and giggled about our co-workers from the department store where we both worked. We had a good laugh at one of our bosses who wore an obvious hairpiece, but mutually hated how he kept hitting on us and the other female staff.

After about twenty minutes, Tina's friends returned and stood before us, dripping. The one wearing white surf shorts faced me directly and asked, "Can you see through these shorts? I'm not wearing any undies, so can you tell me if they are see-through when they're wet?"

What he was actually saying was "Look at my dick."

I didn't want to look at it and thought it was a rather offensive question, but I didn't know how to respond appropriately. They were friends of my friend, and I didn't know what the protocol was. He continued to stand there waiting, so I felt pressured to "check" for him. I braced myself for what I might encounter. I had just been staring out onto the magnificent, sparkling, blue ocean, so the last thing I wanted to look at on such a lovely day was some guy's genitals.

"So can ya see it?" he asked.

"Um . . . I can see some dark hair but that's about all," I truthfully answered with flushing cheeks.

"You sure?" he asked.

What does this jerk want from me? I was not in the mood to be forced to study the area between this wanker's legs any further. I nodded my head.

His mate chuckled and nudged him with his elbow. Then, they both laughed and did some secret handshake thing. After they dried themselves off a bit, they decided to leave.

Good riddance!

About an hour later, Tina and I could both feel that our skin had taken enough beating from the sun, so it was time to leave. We parted ways. She left in one direction, and I took off in the other, heading for the main steps. As I was trudging up towards them, a bronzed surfer with blond hair and a fit physique was changing out of his wet surf shorts under a towel. I glanced over and quietly thought to myself that he looked quite appealing. He noticed me looking at him, and I thought he might offer me a smile as I walked by. He did smile, but as he did, he flashed his towel open and flaunted his "male wares" at me. It was as if I was expected to feel privileged for seeing his manhood, because he seemed quite proud of himself. I looked away immediately and dashed up the sandy path, feeling nothing but disgust and annoyance.

As I walked home along the esplanade, I thought about the first time a male showed me his pecker. I was eight years old and nobody had given me any warning or preparation for it. I certainly had no skills to deal with it when it happened.

The house next door was being built. Two tradesmen, *tradies* as we call them, were working on the site that day. One middle-aged man wearing a dirty pair of overalls was busy laying bricks, and the other, older builder, equally as grubby, was hammering something. I had been there only a minute when the younger of the two approached me, asking me what I was doing.

I noticed dry concrete dust trapped in the prickly growth on his face and thought quietly to myself that he needed a bath. "I'm just looking for a few rocks for my tadpole pond," I answered, feeling rather intimidated by the towering figure.

The scruffy workman slipped a cigarette into his dirty mouth, cupped his hand around the end, put his lighter flame to it, sucked deeply on one end and held his breath as if about to dive underwater. He narrowed his eyes then slowly exhaled a plume of smoke over his head. "What kind do you need?" he questioned.

I demonstrated the size by cupping my hand. I had seen my friend's tadpole tank the day before and liked the rocks she'd put in hers, so that's where I got the idea to rummage through the building site for mine.

"You won't find any out here, but I thought I saw some around the back," he exclaimed. He headed towards the side of the construction, motioning with his finger for me to come.

I followed closely. His muddy work boots crunched the rubble underneath as he stomped heavily along. I trailed behind searching the ground.

When we arrived at the back of the structure, he stopped abruptly. We were now completely isolated from the view of any passers-by, not that I noticed at the time. I continued to scan the ground that was scattered with unacceptable chunks of cement.

"Is *this* what you're looking for?" he asked in an odd sounding tone. When I looked up, he was holding a sausage-shaped object in his hand. It was somewhat stiff, pinkish in colour and the fleshy-looking appendage was poking through the zipper of his pants.

I glanced at it briefly, then up to his face, searching for some degree of clarity. He was grinning, as if something was quietly amusing him, but it seemed creepy. He gestured with his eyes, coercing me to continue looking at it. I did, but only for another second. I realized it wasn't shaped like any rock I'd seen, more like a stick than a rock. "No, that's not the right shape!" I blurted out.

At that moment, the innocence of my youth was both a blessing and a curse. I didn't recognize what this ugly-looking slug was at first, but equally didn't recognize the danger I was in. Without any framework to guide me, I was slow to comprehend just how to react. *What am I supposed to do now? Am I supposed to smirk too? I don't get the joke, is it going to perform a trick? Why does he appear to be so proud of such a stupid-looking thing?*

My head started feeling chaotic, with all sorts of scrambled thoughts buzzing around. I felt "icky." I couldn't explain my emotions but just felt something was wrong. I became overwhelmed with the sudden urge to run home, so I did, abruptly and urgently. "Okay, I'm going home now. Bye," I announced, taking off as fast as my little legs could run.

When I reached the safety of my bedroom, I sat quietly on my bed, hugging my teddy bear, trying to process what had just taken place. After a while, I came to the realization of what I had just been shown. It had to have been a boy part. The rest of what happened continued to remain a mystery. I couldn't really work it out: the smirk, the suggestive tone in his voice, the coercion to have me look, why he wanted me to see it. I didn't get it. All I knew was that I felt dirtied by it.

That evening at dinner with my family, nothing appeared to be any different, except that it was. *I* felt different. It was as if I had been shoved into some kind of premature adulthood that I wasn't ready for, and the events of earlier that day were weighing too heavily on me.

I didn't feel that I could get through dinner without bursting into tears. I simply needed to unload my burdens and knew I had to give the whole thing over to Dad. I had thought that if I told him, then everything, somehow, would be okay. After placing my knife and fork neatly on my plate, I rose up from my chair, stepped quietly over to him and whispered into his ear.

"Daddy, some man showed me his *tossie*." I believe our family were the only people who used that term. His reaction was far greater than I ever anticipated or could have imagined, and I was totally unprepared for the hurricane of fury that exploded.

He immediately shot up from his chair, slammed his hands down hard on the table, rattling everything on it, including two glasses, various pieces of cutlery and the salt and pepper shakers. His face turned the colour of raspberry jam, and his eyes became huge, like the time our pet parrot bit into his finger and wouldn't let go. "What?" he barked with seething rage, frightening us all. I slinked back, nearly wetting myself. "Who? Tell me who it was!" he barked so furiously that I could barely manage to squeak.

"It was the workman next door," I almost apologetically explained.

His eyes flew to Mums, who furrowed her brow with confusion. Dad grabbed the keys out from his pocket.

"Right, into the car now!" he instructed urgently.

Mum loaded me into the car like our vacation luggage, and my eldest sister was put in charge. We sped off.

I was asked to take a seat in a chilly, featureless room. My parents sat in chairs next to me, Dad bouncing his knee anxiously while Mum tightly clutched her bone handbag that she had resting upon her lap. The questions that followed weren't difficult to answer, but disturbing to hear. The two uniformed officers were opening up a world to me that I didn't feel prepared or ready for.

"Do you know what the man was showing you?"

"I think so. It was his tossie." I hated even saying that word, especially to someone outside the family. It just felt so incredibly embarrassing.

"Did the man ask you to touch his tossie?"

"No." I shook my head.

A sad, but friendly looking doll appeared before me, but it wasn't for me to play with. "Did the man touch you in any place on your body? You can point to the place on the dolly if you need to?"

I didn't need to touch the doll, although, I would have liked to have cuddled it.

"Did the man ask you to do anything to him?"

"No." I just wanted to go home. I didn't want to be asked any more of those questions. I was scared and confused and thinking I might be in trouble, because after all, I *was* at the police station. The questions were finally over.

After arriving home that evening, the incident was never spoken about again and there was no significant closure to the event. I don't even remember being comforted or having anything explained to me. All that remained was some kind of disturbance in my brain and a feeling of being inflicted with something that had tarnished me.

* * *

There were others too. That tradesman wasn't the only one who got his thrills exposing himself to minors. There were a few "flashers" who whipped out their goods at me as I walked past, shocking and horrifying my young brain.

One flashed my friend and me in the city, and there was the old bloke on the bus who wouldn't stop staring at me. He pulled his pecker out for me to look at too.

I had no interest in seeing that part of a male or having them flopped out in front of me. All it did was cause me to fear and loathe them. For so many males, it seemed that their sex organs were weapons to frighten, intimidate and violate girls. I had been hearing reports on the news about girls and women being raped and murdered. The crimes always seemed to be motivated by men's sexual urges. That sounded to me like something I didn't want any part of and a reason to steer clear of men altogether.

* * *

When I arrived home from the beach that day, my family were all sitting at the table: my sister, Kerry; her husband, Glen; my other sister, Julie; and my brother, Brett. Julie was there only for a few days. She had moved to the nearby islands to be with her boyfriend shortly after we moved to the Gold Coast. She would regularly fly home for short visits however. My brother had only just arrived after driving up from Melbourne and was about to settle on the coast with the rest of us.

"Well, kids, it's been less than two years since moving up

here, but it has added ten years to my life. I'm sure of it!" Dad knocked on the table with firm conviction. He had assured himself that moving to Queensland was the second-best decision he'd ever made, giving up his booze was the first.

It had been a while since our family had been assembled all together, and although the reunion was pleasant, the relationships with my siblings had always been rather strained. They seemed to enjoy teasing me and picking on me with hurtful cruelties for no reason—or maybe it was because I was the youngest. They could be quite insensitive, and I'm not sure if they were aware just how much at times.

Naturally, this put an involuntary wall up in front of me, and as much as I wanted to be close to them, I never felt that they were capable, or even willing, to be the big sisters and brother I really needed them to be. Despite their teasing, I did love them and enjoyed their company in short bursts. I have always been especially entertained by my brother's jocularity.

After half an hour of catching up, my siblings made their way out into the backyard to dip in the pool and soak up the Queensland sun. I stayed inside with Mum. I was already sunburnt, and I needed to let her know of my plans.

"Mum, I'm going over to Mikey's later," I told her.

"Oh, well if you want to, Love, but don't you want to stick around? Brett's just arrived," she said sunnily, trying to entice me to stay.

"I'll wait and go over after dinner, I haven't seen him in a while."

"Okay, Petal, will you be staying over the night?"

"Maybe. I have a key just in case I come back here later tonight." I assured her I would be safe.

"Okay, Sweetheart." She rose from her chair and carried a handful of plates into the kitchen, placing them on the sink, which she then grabbed on to. I watched her stretch out her back while her face twisted up, her eyes squeezed tight. The pain in her back and legs was clearly agonizing. She had Multiple Sclerosis, and it was evidently becoming worse. I could tell that soon she would be in a wheelchair, and this was going to be one of the last times I would ever see her standing up.

"Go and sit down, Mum," I proposed. "I'll finish the dishes."

She nodded graciously and took up a chair by the window, looking out at the others laughing and splashing about. Her face softened as she delighted in having all the family together around her again.

Chapter 3

"Let's take pictures of us having sex!"

My breath hitched under my diaphragm. "What? No!" I had no control over my reaction.

"Why not?" Mikey replied.

"I just don't want to, that's all."

"Oh geez, you act like such a baby sometimes," he retorted as he sat up in the bed, crossing his arms in annoyance. It wasn't the first sexual fantasy of Mikey's that I'd ruined and probably wasn't going to be the last. I realized there was definitely something deeply entrenched in me that was behind my immediate refusal.

It seemed that when it came to sex play in the bedroom, I became scared, anxious and confused. I was unsure what was considered normal and what wasn't. It was becoming obvious to me that I was damaged from my formative years, and the expression of my scarring rushed forth the moment he suggested taking the pictures. Doing anything that appeared to be out of the realm of "love making" frightened me. I couldn't possibly explain it. It all struggled on my lips, and he wouldn't understand anyway. I had to try to appeal to the softer part of him I hoped was there.

"I'm sorry, Mikey, could we please just snuggle for tonight?" I cringed in anticipation of a hostile response. To my pleasant surprise, I was met with as much as he could give, an eye-rolling, and an outstretched arm, complete with a heavy sigh as if to say, "If we must." There weren't many times he offered to be affectionate, so I took what I could get.

As I lay in the soft warmth of his arms, my mind drifted back to a time in my adolescence, thinking to myself that perhaps one specific event may be what caused my reaction.

* * *

When it came to having my picture taken, my much older

cousin, Derek, was the one I remember being behind the lens. He took hundreds of family snaps of us as we were growing up and was regularly taking me aside for our own *special* photo sessions. His passion for photography, and the fact that I was the youngest, and therefore the cutest, were what I assumed was his justification for frequently singling me out. I was only half right.

The first time I recall being ill at ease with him, was when I was fourteen, the same year I was also dealing with my neighbour's peering eye. It may have been sooner though, as I have a vivid recollection of someone who sounded just like him, sneaking into my room late at night when I was around seven or eight years old. Somebody pulled back my blanket, lifted up my pyjama top, caressed my bare tummy and whispered, "You're a little cutie aren't you!" It was a male voice, most definitely without question.

The arousal in his tone and the touch of those fingertips tracing over my skin and tickling me in that way alarmed me into a panicked, rigid fright. I was left completely terrified and feeling there was something extremely wrong about it. It was one of those spine-chilling moments in one's life that you never forget and can still relive like it was yesterday.

I never told anyone. I didn't know if I should. Over the years, I narrowed it down to only two people it could have been that night, and it has basically come down to a hunch, going by the sound of the voice.

* * *

When I was fourteen, I stayed at my cousin's flat for four days of babysitting his eighteen-month-old son. He had requested me specifically, asking Mum if I could stay there while his much younger wife was in hospital having their second baby. He had me desperately yearning for home after my first night.

After settling the precious, powdery tot down for the

evening, I joined Derek in the living room and nestled into one of the spare lounge chairs. I was expecting something on the television to entertain me but can recall the news being on. Derek glanced over the top of his newspaper from a matching chair two feet away, and I reassured him that all was well with his son.

An oversized pine bookcase in the center of the room commanded my attention. It shelved many of his books, most of them quite sizeable and impressive to my eyes. Upon my mere mention of his collection, Derek leaped up from his chair and bounded towards the piece. He reached for a large, heavy-looking book that had a glossy cover and rushed back to my chair with it. He sat himself down on the arm of the chair and opened the book, balancing it on his knees. He was smiling from ear to ear, and I didn't know why. His fingers began flipping through the pages, which were full of photographs. He was searching for a specific page. He'd stopped somewhere around the middle.

"Oh here they are! These photos are gorgeous. Have a look at these. They are just stunning!" he exclaimed.

The lustrous, oversized photographs now shoved under my nose showed adolescent girls who were posed completely naked. Their ages appeared similar to mine, some younger, perhaps eleven or twelve years old. They were all standing there without a stitch of clothing. He flipped over the pages, slowly and carefully, making sure I saw everything thoroughly. They were more of the same thing, young girls standing facing the lens with no clothes on.

"See how gorgeous they are?" he coerced me to agree.

That was the first time I had seen nude photos of any kind. The girls stood facing forward with barely any development to their unclothed bodies, flat chested, little or no pubic hair, unenhanced by makeup and expressionless. Some were in groups of two or three, some standing alone, all photographed in black and white. I was shocked and confused.

He left me with the opened book on my lap, saying, "It would really benefit you to study these photos, see how stunning they look? That is real art!"

How on earth will this benefit me?

He leaped back over to his showcase library he appeared to be so proud of and starting thumbing through more pages of other similar-looking books. Perhaps he was trying to find even more pictures to show me. At that point, I remember my stomach started to churn, and the delicate, warming sensations that I had felt from the purity of his infant son only five minutes earlier had all but vanished.

This doesn't feel right. Why would my own cousin want me to see these pictures? And why is he acting so excited over them? I snapped the book shut, feeling overwhelmed by a strange and unusual feeling of annoyance, offence and betrayal, but I didn't understand those feelings at the time, despite desperately trying to.

I willed my eyes to absorb my tears from the abuse of my innocence and trust. The last thing I wanted to do was to cry in front of him. For one, I didn't want to appear overly immature; and secondly, I didn't want to let on that I had never seen nudity before, although I had no idea why I felt that way. All I knew was that I needed a distraction and quickly.

I rose from my chair, walked over to the TV set and started turning the dial, searching the stations for something that would divert his attention away from anything else he may have been planning.

Observing my complete disinterest, Derek returned to his newspaper, most likely disappointed he got no reaction from me. Regardless, I do recall him having a lingering grin that I didn't understand. I had seen that same lecherous type of secret grin on somebody else before.

The events of that evening caused me to lie awake rigidly until dawn. In my sleeplessness, I felt tormented by the feeling of being shoved into a world reserved only for grown-ups, one that I knew it was wrong for me to be in. I desperately ached for the cozy solace of my own bed.

Around noon the next day, exhausted from not sleeping, I was able to put the baby down for his nap. It was then that Derek told me that he wanted to take photos of me outside. I worried immediately that he wanted to pose me like those girls in the photo book, and that's why he encouraged me to "study them for my benefit." On the other hand, he had taken many photos of us previously without incident, so I dismissed my concern and trusted him. *He wouldn't cause me any harm, surely. He is family.*

"Okay, try to relax and smile," he instructed with his familiar friendly, yet professional approach.

I sat awkwardly on the back stoop. Although I was used to sitting in front of his lens over the years, I was no longer a young child and was feeling particularly self-conscious. This had been intensified by having my neighbour watching me that year, and I was becoming very self-aware and protective of my body.

He clicked his shutter as many times as it took until he could sense I was becoming more relaxed. Bored was more like it.

"Good, okay, now how about you undo the top button of your shirt," he suggested brazenly. His tone was flat and factual, as if revealing yourself was an industry standard for modeling.

I froze with a fearful hesitation. *Was he serious?*

"It will look sexy, I promise!" he reassured.

What does "sexy" mean? Does he think those naked girls in those photos are "sexy"? I don't think I want to be "sexy."

He gestured encouragingly, again cajoling me into something I wasn't ready for. Acting against my gut trying to tell me not to, I lifted my hand to the button of the shirt, stalling over it.

"It's okay. Trust me," he said, his mouth turning upwards at the corners.

Reluctantly, I did as instructed, but after undoing the button, I adjusted the shirt in the attempt to keep any part of my chest hidden. My chest hadn't developed that much, but what little I had was not for anyone to gawk at, neither my cousin nor my neighbour.

He pressed the shiny button on the top of his camera. "Great!" he chuffed, cocking his head sideways and examining me more thoroughly. His hazel eyes surveyed me up and down slowly. "You look great, absolutely beautiful! Okay, now how about you take off that shirt. It will look fantastic!"

Every vein in my body instantly surged with a searing, prickly heat of sheer terror, although I couldn't let on. I shook my head "No" vigorously. I could feel my cheeks burn.

"Okay, what about if you take off the shirt, but you can cover yourself up with this," he said, handing me a small hand towel.

I found it odd at the time that he just happened to have it on hand, making its sudden appearance onto the scene. I stiffened and hesitated.

"It's okay. Take this towel and cover yourself up if you want to, but it will just look much better without the shirt. Trust me!" he urged, handing me the towel.

I again, reluctantly did what he wanted me to, and I removed my shirt slowly and carefully, placing the towel over me as much as I could manage. It was all so awkward. I was clumsy and felt like I was burning inside with fire. It was the beginning of me loathing him for what he was doing, but I didn't understand what I was experiencing and was overwhelmed with too many feelings at once.

I sat how he wanted me to, holding the towel over my chest, and forced a smile, but I really wanted to cry. He snapped a couple of shots.

"Okay, how about you lie down on the grass and take away the towel" The mere utterance of the words paralysed me. I immediately shook my head "No" again.

"Are you sure? It looks good!" he pressed further.

I nodded again, becoming desperate for my mother's safe arms. He reassured me it would be fine, and it was "artistic." My gut was saying not to, but I ignored it again, trusting him instead. I lay down as he instructed but kept the towel covering me. He snapped his camera again, clicking and taking photos.

"So how about taking away the towel?" he said. "It will be beautiful, artistic and very sexy."

I became not only irritated with his persistence, but also upset almost to the point of bursting with angry, hot tears. I believe at that point, he could finally see that he had reached the limit of his requests.

Don't cry, don't cry, whatever you do, don't cry.

"Okay, well we've probably got enough shots for now," he surrendered.

I breathed a breath of gratitude and silently whispered, "Thank You" towards the sky. It was a tremendous relief when I finally got to leave that place and go home to my family.

I never told anybody what took place, foolishly second-guessing myself about the whole thing. I tried to reason that because he was an older and well-respected family member, someone everybody admired, that perhaps I might have misread the situation. I had heard about girls who spoke up about things like that, and their bravery backfired very badly. Naturally, I didn't want anything like that to happen. I didn't want to be the cause any problems or rifts in the family. I certainly didn't want to be blamed for being a troublemaker just in case I *was* wrong. Never once did I consider myself a victim of child abuse. How could I have understood that's what it was? I couldn't have. I was too young and trusted him instead of my instincts.

* * *

His visits continued over the years, his trusty camera always in hand and taking family snaps when he came to see us. When I turned sixteen and was attending business college, he requested that I accompany him for a "professional" photo session.

The story he had my mother and father believe, was that he would take me to a well-known beach in Chelsea and take photos of me for a reputable, well-known photographic company, potentially launching me in a modeling career.

This was the first I'd heard of any such thing and had never given any thought to becoming any kind of model, so I didn't care one way or the other. Mum and Dad didn't seem to have much reason to object, except that I'd miss half a day of college. We all basically agreed only because Derek seemed so excited about it. I had not forgotten about what happened just two years earlier, but I deflected any doubt for the sake of family loyalty. I was instructed to bring a couple of changes of outfits and swimwear.

It took us a few hours to drive to the shoreline and a further fifteen minutes trudging along the sand, carrying all the gear, looking for the perfect spot. He was finally happy with a secluded part of the beach and being that it was midweek, there was barely anybody around for miles.

"Okay, now I want you to pose like a real model for me," he requested.

My mind went completely blank. "Could you tell me exactly how you want me?" I needed his experience, as he made his living as a photographer, so I assumed he would have known how to pose his models.

"Oh, you know, just stand how the girls do in the magazines."

My mind still drew a blank.

"I'm not sure how," I tried explaining, shrugging my shoulders.

"Okay, just do what comes naturally," he smiled. By that point, I suspected he was just as clueless as I was.

He clicked his shutter regardless of how stupidly I posed and told me I looked good anyway. I still felt somewhat nervous, and it took me a good while to relax, but by my third bathing suit change, under the protection of a large beach towel, I slowly became more at ease. The moment he could see I had become relaxed, he seized his window of opportunity.

"Great, now how about you take off your top?" His request was bold and unashamed.

My reaction was no different than the first time he asked me, two years ago. A hot rush of panic and confusion surged within me. I refused without a moment's hesitation and shook my head "No."

"Are you sure? It looks really nice, *really* nice!" He urged me further.

It didn't take much to get me to the point of agitation, and I was definitely feeling violated. I shook my head again. "I think I want to go home," I told him.

"Already? Why? Aren't you enjoying the beach?" he questioned, taking the weight of his camera up with his free hand.

"I'm getting a headache," I exaggerated. My tone was apologetic, yet with impatience. I wanted to leave. I didn't feel like being subjected to any more of this perverted force a moment longer. *I'm his cousin, I don't get it! What's with the nudity? I'm still too young for this. This is wrong.*

He shrugged his shoulders, "Okay, well if you want to go, I suppose so."

I started gathering the gear before he had the chance to try to change my mind. I wasn't sure whether he wanted to get me completely naked or goodness knows what, but I didn't want to stick around to find out. Never again would I go anywhere alone with this guy, and the respect and admiration I once felt had all but crumbled into a pile of ash.

As I became caught up in clouded confusion in the days and weeks following, I foolishly let it all go, again, thinking only of him and his reputation and not about myself. My gut kept twisting and nudging at me, trying to urge me to speak up, but I suppressed it all, fearful of the outcome. That is what predators count on.

* * *

Mikey had fallen fast asleep. I didn't want to wake him, so I turned and faced the other way, alone with my thoughts. I tried to fit the pieces of my past together in a way that made sense. I needed to know who I was and why I reacted the way I did. I needed to try to understand where I was sexually.

Will I ever get the chance to discover my sexuality at my own pace? When I'm *ready and not being continually forced into things?* I recalled my first boyfriend rushing me into losing my virginity when I wasn't ready.

Will I ever get a chance to repair any of the damage already done? I closed my eyes but didn't sleep for hours, worried and anxious that I was ruined somehow.

Chapter 4

The early morning warbling from a family of magpies gently woke us around eight o'clock. Mikey propped himself against the wall with his pillow. "I want you to move in with me," he stated bluntly, eyes soft.

"Huh?" I queried so eloquently, rubbing the crusty sleep from my eyes.

"Yep, you move in with me, and we can go halves in the costs."

Gee, well if he puts it that way, how can a girl resist? "Okay," I agreed pragmatically. I was anxious to get away from Dad's difficult moods, and this provided me with the perfect avenue to escape. I was going to have to tell my parents that I would be moving out again. *I wonder how they are going to take it? I have only been back home for a few months.*

When we had first moved to the Gold Coast two years earlier, I lived with my parents in their new house for the first year. Julie, my middle sister, moved straight from our family home in Melbourne to the Pacific Islands for a man who lured her with the promise of an exciting life in another part of the world. She couldn't resist, I suppose. My oldest sister, Kerry, married an older guy, Glen, and they settled on the coast. My brother, Brett, stayed behind in Melbourne for a couple of years and had only now joined us, moving into a nearby flat. My boyfriend, Mitchell, who I'd been with since I was fifteen, had moved up to be with me. He had found his own flat close by with another boy his age.

After my eighteenth birthday, Mitchell started becoming serious and began talking about engagement. The mere thought completely rattled me. *Is my life going to be over before it has even begun?* I instantly pictured a life tied to a kitchen sink and thrown into motherhood way too early with no chance to live or travel or experience the world. I had this misguided hope that life was going to offer me something dazzling, filled with thrills and excitement. I didn't like the thought of being married and tied down one bit.

Instead of letting his informal proposal down gently and just keeping things the way they were, I broke up with him. Marriage was way down the track, in a distant place in the farthest reaches of my plans, so I panicked.

It broke my heart to let him go. Mitchell was my first love, and I was his. He was a nice boy who I met at church, and he was just as clumsy and clueless about sex as I was. He did rush me into it though. I guess his hormones were raging more crazily than mine were. I succumbed to his pressure because I loved him, a common mistake we girls make at that age. Managing just the basics was about all we could handle. There was certainly never anything kinky going on, and most of the time we just kissed. My family really liked him, and he was considered one of our family.

After the break up, it took me a while to adjust to everything: the move, being away from my friends, unfamiliar surroundings, having to make a new life, my siblings being all dispersed, our family dog being put down. I felt as though my comfort rug had been pulled out from underneath me, and it was stressful and daunting, despite how beautiful our new town was.

I found myself alone with my parents for the first time. Living with mum was a cinch. She was, and still is, an angel. I love her dearly. Her Multiple Sclerosis, although distressing and painful for her, and heartbreaking to see her suffer through, taught me to become a self-sufficient young woman.

Dad, on the other hand, wasn't so easy. When alcoholics stop drinking, they may lose the bottle, but they retain all of the cantankerous characteristics of a full-time boozer, which laboured the love of our family and tested our patience many times.

After that first year on the coast living with my parents, I was quite anxious to leave the nest. I wanted to get away and begin this wonderful life I'd planned for myself, one of great adventures, excitement, travel and amazing opportunities. I ended up running back with my tail between my legs before the year was up.

Living out of home didn't turn out to be the liberating or thrilling experience I was anticipating, far from it. What sent me back to my parents was the treatment I received from my male flatmates, or more to the point, *mistreatment*. I moved three times in that first year and experienced the same thing each time, sexual assault and violation.

* * *

The first people I shared a flat with were a couple I had known for a few months, Samantha and her boyfriend, Pete. Neither of them worked, so they would sit around all day doing nothing, collecting government handouts, being unmotivated and dull. I worked during the day, so I didn't have to spend too much time in their company. That was until Pete started entering my bedroom at night.

Every other evening, once Samantha and I had turned in, Pete would open my door *while* knocking on it, with one of his flimsy, pre-planned excuses. He had to check that my window was closed, ostensibly "a security measure," or to make sure I had turned on my alarm clock, or to see if I had enough blankets. Sometimes he claimed he'd heard a noise. His justifications seemed endless. "I have to look after my girls!" he would proclaim.

I hated his intrusions but felt powerless. *How do I handle this? What do I do? What do I say?*

One night after he entered my room, unconvincingly concerned about the security of my window, he sauntered towards me and impudently sat on the edge of my bed. His breath smelled strongly of coffee, which repelled me. He asked if I needed some water.

"No thanks!" the volume of my reply caused him to place

one of his fingers on my lips, hushing them. He lowered to a whisper, urging me to follow his lead. When I looked into his eyes, I noticed they were almost black, yet twinkled with something felonious, threatening almost. He studied my face carefully. I couldn't tell what he was thinking.

"Okay, then, well goodnight," he said, as he leaned over and pressed his hard mouth onto mine. He immediately offered me his tongue.

I pulled back with an immediate reaction of disgust. I felt an instant pang of guilt and remorse for *cheating* on my friend, yet it appeared that he did not share the same culpability.

In my naivety and my strange fear of potentially angering males if I rejected them, I tried to maintain some level of politeness. At the same time, I still had to get my message of disinterest across. I hated being put in that position.

"Goodnight, then," I replied, rolling over and turning my back to him. He could see then that he wasn't going to get what he wanted that night.

He left me with a tremendous weight on my shoulders: faultless guilt towards my friend, anger at his lack of contrition, and fear from the violation of his constant intrusions upon my privacy, my personal space and my physical being.

He returned a few nights later, then a few nights after that, and then a few more times, doing similar things and becoming even more audacious each time. Over the weeks and months he had lain beside me while trying to start up "nighttime chats," attempted to climb under the blankets with me complaining of the cold—it was *never* cold on the coast—stroked my hair, offered me back and neck rubs and frequently tried kissing me.

I was always afraid of his advances, yet still somehow felt I had to maintain a small courtesy towards him. I don't know how I managed it, but the entire time I remained politely unyielding to his desires. Maybe it was my father's temper and the many news reports I'd seen about violent rapes and aggravated assaults upon women that cultivated my very real fear and mistrust in men. I genuinely believed, with every morsel of my being, that each and every one of them, given the right conditions, could snap instantly. I had heard stories of girls and women who rejected the advances of males and ended up in hospital, bruised and battered. Sometimes they didn't even make it *that* far. I feared that level of physical violence happening to me.

With that fear and inexperience of youth, I lacked the confidence to handle the situation the way I should have. I was absolutely terrified to assert myself. I had never been taught how to be direct or assertive. I just didn't possess the fortitude to say, "Get lost!" or even better, "Back off jerk or I'll tell your girlfriend!"

The only defence I thought I had against my intruder was to give him the message subtly without antagonizing him. I tried door barricades, wearing more to bed, changing my sleep times, keeping Samantha up late taking, avoiding eye contact and never allowing him the chance to get me alone. Keeping the wolf from the door was exhausting, and after a few months, I'd had truly had enough. I needed an escape plan.

Are all men predators, cheaters and liars? Is sex the only thing they care about? In their lustful desires, do they not consider their female prey and how she *feels about their advances? Do they not care about the repercussions of their behaviour? Does it even occur to them that their girlfriends would be heartbroken?* How they seemed completely unconcerned about anyone or anything but getting their own rocks off was completely baffling to me. *Surely not all of them are like that, are they?*

* * *

It took less than a week to be offered another room in

another share flat, and being desperate to escape my current living conditions, I recklessly took up the offer. It didn't dawn on me at the time that I had just agreed to share with two males, and that I may find twice as much trouble.

At first it seemed fine. I barely saw one of them, Tony, only occasionally running into him in the hall or the kitchen. His eyes were always bloodshot; he made no sense when he talked, and he smelled like a bushfire most of the time. I suspected he was smoking pot.

I saw my other flatmate, Mark, more often. He was a keen surfer, fit and tanned, nice looking—a typical *coastie*. He adorned himself in spiritual charms and spoke of chakras and gurus and offered to do something called *reiki* on me. I declined politely. Not only was I afraid of the sound of it, but I also didn't want him touching me too intimately.

At the beginning of the fifth week, Mark invited me into his bedroom. He wanted to show me something that was in there. I followed him in without suspicion.

"What is it?" I asked, looking about the room.

I was completely unprepared for what was about to happen. He shut the door, which instantly struck me as odd, then grabbed both my hands and began walking backward, leading me towards his bed. He then sat down on it. With his hands holding mine, I had no option but to stand before him.

"What are you doing?" I asked, worried.

"I've seen the way you look at me. I know you want me, and I have something for you," he alluded to his crotch with his eyes.

"Yeah, right, let me go," I scoffed, desperately hoping he was kidding.

"Don't laugh. This is what you do to me, and I think you need to do something about it," he told me.

I quickly scanned his face, searching for any hint of jest, but from the expectancy in his eyes and his lip-biting smirk, the realization hit me hard. I could feel myself being pulled down, as if I were in an undercurrent of dread and fear, but it was Mark, tugging me onto my knees. I struggled against the pressure of his hands upon my shoulders, trying to stay on my feet, but I was no match for his strength.

"Oh no, you're not going anywhere, missy!" he announced.

An intense, hot fear filled me entirely. I became desperate to understand what I had done to cause this colossal misunderstanding. *I might have shot him a quick glance here and there when he wasn't looking, but I certainly never gave out any signals and most definitely never asked for this!* It appeared that he had convinced himself I had invited his advances.

"You know you want it," he progressed, gesturing his crotch to me.

"Let me go, Mark, this isn't funny!" I didn't want to give too much of my real fear away to him, because he could use that to his advantage.

"Oh aren't you the feisty one!" he chuffed, leaning down to kiss my mouth.

I turned my head away so his lips landed on the top of my head. He tried again, and again I moved my head. The last thing I wanted was for his disgusting lips to touch me, so I continued to wriggle about.

He gave up trying to kiss me and started fiddling with his zipper. Any second, his pecker would be out, and I would be expected to . . . *My shoulders, he let go of one of my shoulders!*

I took the brief opportunity to get out from his clutches and bolt for the door. In one swift movement, I sprang up and ran for it. I turned the knob and flung the door open, fleeing swiftly out into the hall and down into my bedroom, slamming my door shut. The door had no lock, so all I could do was pray to anyone who would listen that he wouldn't follow me. I sat up straight shouldered on my bed and readied myself in a battle position.

I trembled, barely able to find a substantial breath to calm myself. My heart pounded heavily, as if it were pulverizing my lungs, almost causing them to malfunction. My mind raced. *How on earth did he ever get the idea that I deserved or wanted him that way? Whatever he took from my glimpses, he has obviously blown it way out of proportion and assumed I was having some kind of perverted fantasy about him. No, that's not what I was thinking at all!*

His decision against pursuing me further that night was a tremendous relief. Perhaps my reaction had bruised his precious ego. Maybe he realized he was mistaken after all. I didn't care. I was just glad he left me alone that night.

I feared him now. He could decide to advance on me at any time, dragging me to my knees, becoming even more forceful. No, I couldn't stay there; I had to find a safer environment.

* * *

John and Adrian were acquaintances of mine from around the coast, both in their early twenties and looking for a flatmate. I again hastily took the room without thinking.

Over the weeks and months, I tolerated their silly games and childish antics. I had to duck while they kicked their ball around, sidestep their rough and tumble games, and put up with Playboy centrefolds pinned up all over the walls and stinking beer bottles lying about. I also suffered the constant stench of what smelled like bushfire, wafting out from under their doorways, which made me feel queasy. Their blaring rock music would crash and smash its way into my morning sleep-in on the weekends, and the revving of their engines as they tinkered on their cars constantly tested my patience.

One afternoon, I came home from work to find a magazine on my bed. I was in no way prepared for what I was about to be exposed to. After picking up the unfamiliar publication, I looked at the front cover and saw a picture of a young lady standing naked next to a horse. *What the heck is this?*

I opened up the pages and vomit instantly reached the

back of my throat. Page after page showed pictures of naked girls doing sexual things . . . to animals! I was thunderstruck!

I reached the toilet just in time, lifting the seat and throwing up everything I had eaten that day. Having never even seen "normal" pornography before, I was in no way prepared for that level of twisted sickness. I adored and revered all animals, and it repulsed me to see any ill treatment of God's innocent creatures. Once you see something like that, you can never *unsee* it. I chucked the magazine from my room into the hallway and slammed my door, furious and disillusioned with not only them but *all* males.

John and Adrian naturally thought it was hilarious, and my anger at them didn't slow down their boisterous behaviour. They continued their juvenile capers, as if stirring me up was some kind of warped mission. One night they decided to push me even further.

It might have started out as fun and games for them, but it escalated to something much more serious, causing me to reach my limit and storm out then and there.

The three of us had been watching some silly movie I wasn't paying much attention to. The premise of the film was a girl having two male friends, and the three of them ended up in bed together in the end. It wasn't sexually explicit, nor was it overly graphic. Once it ended, I rose from my chair and headed for the kitchen to make a cup of tea. John and Adrian then both shot up from their seats and completely ambushed me, sandwiching me between them. They pressed their bodies hard up against me. Adrian was in front of me and John was behind.

"What's going on?" I cried out with surprising volume.

"Oh you want a threesome with us, don't you!" they chuckled.

"Come on. Show us your vagina," John added.

I was terrified! They both had me pinned in between them, and there was no way out. They rubbed their groins against me, saying, "You want us, don't you? Ooh yeah, baby. You want our hard dicks don't you!"

Their rowdy laughter was my only saving grace, for as long as they were treating this as a joke, I thought I still had a slim chance of getting out of this fairly unharmed. I wriggled and struggled.

"Let me go!" I yelled while pushing and kicking, but to no avail. They had me tightly in their grasp.

John, being the brawnier of the two, had a vice grip on my arms, restraining them behind my back, his rough nails digging into my skin. Adrian, who was lesser in stature, but not without his own strength, ripped my shirt open, exposing my bra.

"Oooh, nice titties!" Adrian exclaimed, eyes widening.

I struggled harder, kicking at him with my feet, but he jumped back each time. He grabbed my breasts, squeezing them hard.

My heart pounded in terror, my breath almost all expelled from the exhaustion of fighting. A real panic had risen up inside me. *They aren't kidding around anymore.* I glared at him venomously.

"Oh yeah, baby, very nice titties you have there!" Adrian continued, his eyes now displaying a lustful hunger. His playfulness had become serious, and I was in trouble. He eyed John and nodded and winked at him. It was as if they had some kind of secret boy code I didn't understand, because John was then given the go-ahead for his turn.

John released one of my arms in order to then grab my behind, and as he squeezed my backside, I managed to elbow him in his chest. "Aww!" he chortled. "Now, come on. Don't be like that. We can do this the easy way or the hard way."

"*No* way!" I hollered, trying to sound serious yet without angering them.

"You know you're not getting out of here without at least giving us head, don't you?" Adrian wickedly stated.

His words filled me with such terror that I didn't think

about anything but trying to get away. I kicked Adrian so hard in the knee that he stumbled. With every bit of strength I could muster, I reefed my hand out of John's clutches and broke free. I didn't hesitate for a moment, taking that slim opportunity to escape. I slipped up the hall into my bedroom, slamming the door. *I can't believe I am being put through this again!*

Filled with nervous adrenalin, I grabbed my purse and keys and stormed out through the back door, jumping into my car that I briefly had that year, and drove away. I was way too shaken to drive very far, so when I reached the beach two minutes later, I stopped and turned off the engine.

The tears that followed came quickly. *Those bloody idiots have no idea how frightening that was, nor do they have any respect for my human rights. I feel so violated and angry I could scream! Stupid oversexed males, I'm so over this shit.*

When I returned later that evening, I packed up my things quietly, and the next morning I was gone. I returned to the safety of my parent's home for an indeterminate period of much needed convalescence.

A few months later, I started dating Mikey, a nice guy I met at work. I didn't plan on dating anyone at that stage, but he charmed me, not with looks, but with his fun, upbeat personality. I came around to the idea of having a new guy in my life. It seemed I needed someone to protect me from other stupid males. I also hoped that he could share the same dreams and make exciting life plans together.

Now he had asked me to move in with him, and I had to tell my parents that I was moving out again. *What am I getting myself into?*

Chapter 5

A slight jiggling of the bed woke me. It was Mikey's hands fumbling under the mattress. He pulled out a large plastic baggie containing a grassy substance and slipped quietly out of the room. I recognized the look and smell of dope but detested the stuff. Almost every male I had known smoked it. He had obviously been hiding his habit from me. It was common for pot smokers to do that. If they were with a person who they knew didn't smoke it or like the stuff, they figured it was easier to try to hide it than be honest. From the considerable amount that was in that bag, it didn't appear to be all for him.

I heard two male voices mumbling in the kitchen. One belonged to Mikey, but I couldn't place the other. *Oh our first visitor in our new place!* I slipped out of bed, wrapped myself in my pink terry robe, smoothed my hair and went out to greet our guest.

With an urgent flurry of movement, desperate hands tried to conceal a bounty of dope and money that was spread out all over our kitchen counter. I didn't know who that guy was, but he appeared to be buying drugs from my boyfriend. *Oh my goodness, I've just moved in with a drug dealer!*

"Is she cool, man?" the towheaded stranger asked Mikey.

"Yeah, she's okay," he answered for me.

I'm not actually, but thanks for discussing it with me. I certainly wasn't overjoyed to discover that my boyfriend was dealing this stupid stuff.

"I don't like this, Mikey," I said.

He just shrugged. I got myself ready for work and left, disappointed and upset.

The walk to work, twenty minutes at a brisk pace, would give me the opportunity to process how I was going to deal with what I'd just discovered. Walking to work, however, like walking *anywhere* on the coast, brought the usual onslaught of harassment along with it. I largely ignored it all, yet again.

The advantage to moving to the most beautiful part of Australia was the privilege of living alongside miles of pristine coastline with pure white sand and a rich blue ocean that sparkled like diamonds from the sun. Our Gold Coast streets were always spotless and lined with palm trees that swayed in the balmy breezes. Our waterways snaked through our suburbs with multi-million dollar properties taking up their prized executive positions on their banks. The humid air smelled sweet with the fragrance of frangipanis, and with our relaxed atmosphere, warm climate, theme parks and nearby rainforests, it was quickly becoming one of the world's most famous tourist meccas. The postcard-perfect surrounds appealed to me mightily, and I felt very much at home—that was, until I walked around anywhere by myself.

The disadvantage of being an Aussie beach chick was that when I did go out anywhere alone, I became vulnerable to the onslaught of street harassment from every Australian male who passed me by. It didn't matter where I went or what I wore, from light summer clothing through to baggy T-shirts and sweat pants, it was as though I had no right to walk the streets without being a target of sexually charged harassment.

It didn't only happen on the coast. I remember being harassed back in Melbourne starting at around the age of thirteen. The odd car would honk as it drove past, and some bloke would whistle at me, which I didn't like. If I said anything to either one of my sisters, I was just told to take as a *compliment*. I tried to at first, but the car toots and whistles increased in both frequency and intensity with every year, and it really started to wear me down.

When I turned seventeen and first moved to the coast, the harassment increased tremendously, and I soon had all manner of men, of all ages, whistling, tooting and yelling out at me. Their comments were sexist, lewd and really quite vile.

"Hey baby, show us your pink bits!"

"Hey baby, wiggle that hot ass. You're getting us hard!"

The invidious comments weren't exclusive to Australian men, but they certainly were responsible for the crudest of them. Men anywhere from sixteen to seventy-six were all taking part in objectifying not only me, but many other women, my friends included. The very worst of it would usually come from the young Aussie men in their late teens and early twenties, who had absolutely no idea how to behave in public, especially in front of a lady.

There were also the physical assaults. If I was standing in a busy store or crowded place, especially on public transport, I would have my bottom pinched, my breasts groped, crotches rubbed against me, and propositions for sex and other lewd and vile remarks whispered in my ear. When I was at work, I had guys leaping over the counter to kiss my cheek or smell my neck, and I was hit on continually.

Quite often, I was followed by males who would make disgusting remarks.

"Ooh, baby, ya look like ya need big cock in ya!"

"Come on, baby. Flash us your tits!"

"Oh, baby, I'd like some of your tail!"

"You get me horny!"

"How about a head job?"

"Come on, baby. Suck it for me!"

"Ooh, baby, nice ass!"

"Show us your tits!"

"Hey baby, how much?"

"Bend over, sugar. I'll give you a ride!"

"You get my cock hard!"

These so-called *compliments* were never something I found cute, funny or complimentary, but rather insulting, intimidating, abusive, rude, insensitive and vulgar. No woman deserves it, and it wasn't something I should have expected because I was born female.

Many leered and snickered and called me over like a dog. Some would grab their crotches and ask me if I wanted some.

They whistled, hooted and hollered and made sexual gestures with their hands, fingers, mouths and tongues.

Driving a car often became dangerous because of the aggressive and risky manoeuvres males would make trying to catch my attention. They sped up, slowed down, blocked me in and hung out of their windows, whistling and hollering out at me, weaving their cars into my path. I was in constant fear of being driven off the road and crashing into something.

I never did anything to encourage their behaviour or attention. I did not wear anything too tight or too revealing. I didn't wiggle anything, fall out of anything or show off in any way. I didn't even toss my hair in anybody's direction. None of this mistreatment was because of anything I did to attract it. My only crime was simply developing into a young woman.

Whenever I walked out onto the street, I felt objectified, degraded and humiliated in public, as if my intellect, my capabilities as a person or anything I might accomplish in life didn't matter. Nor did any of my hopes, my dreams or my plans for my future. What only seemed to be important to them was how my appearance or sex appeal rated on their scales. They showed no concern about my feelings or whether what they yelled out hurt me. It seemed they expected me to be empty inside, to be the grateful recipient of their male lust.

It was exhausting being continually reminded that I was under constant observation and scrutiny, being evaluated and judged on my appearance. Despite what they thought, being attractive was not the sole purpose for my existence, and my secret wish was to yell at every single one of them, *I am not your dog that you whistle for; I'm not a stray animal you call over, and I am not, I never have been, nor will I ever be, your "baby"!*

My formative years never included any instruction on how to deal with harassment. It just wasn't something anybody discussed or worried about. We were largely left to our own devices and told just to ignore it or accept it as part of our Australian, male-dominated culture.

Mikey wasn't as bad as most young males, but he was certainly a long way from being the guy I was hoping for. After my walk to work, I decided to ignore the drug dealing as best I could. I stuck it out for almost two years.

* * *

One day I discovered that Mikey had been cheating on me. Not only did he cheat, but one girl fell pregnant to him. He frequently flirted with girls, and I knew he kissed at least a few—one on a company picnic that he admitted to—but who knows what else he might have been doing behind my back. This was obviously a deal breaker.

Something shifts inside you when your guy cheats on you, and there's no real coming back from that. I wasn't at all happy about the betrayal, especially in such a crippling way, but at least I could now go out and start living the life I really wanted to, instead of wasting my time with him. I had life to discover, places to travel, nature to marvel at and great opportunities I was probably missing out on. All he seemed interested in was dope and his stupid sex games, none of which I ever became comfortable with. I still wasn't sure whether it was a problem derived from everything males had put me through, or whether I just didn't want to do those things with him. I still had so much to process about myself that way.

Moving back to my parents wasn't an option. My mother, being unable to walk another step, now needed a wheelchair. Both she and my father decided to downsize to a smaller place. They sold our three-bedroom house in Mermaid Beach and bought a small one-bedroom apartment in a luxury complex just on the outskirts of Surfers Paradise, our main tourist hub and the central part of the coast. Dad then took on the role of her full-time caregiver. Even if I wanted to, I couldn't live with them. There wasn't room. I was forced to make it on my own, permanently.

My brother took me in for a brief period until I got on my feet. He had started up a local business and just purchased a two-bedroom beach shack. I was grateful for the room and relieved that he was too busy to put me under his usual scrutiny. I wasn't in the mood for answering his endless drill of questioning.

In a few weeks, I managed to find another job, a cheap, but working car, and some new friends. One girl my age, Natalie, who I met through workmates, mentioned she was looking to move out of her flat, so we decided to share a small place together. I owed it to myself to try living in a drug-free, male-free, safe, non-toxic environment. Didn't I?

Chapter 6

Natalie was a good-time girl, finding her happiness in embracing the party lifestyle, rather than becoming a tree hugger like me. My enjoyment of nature and the wonders of the universe didn't interest her in the slightest. Talking about boys and being obsessive about her looks was the limit of her concerns. All of her slap and fuss wasn't at all necessary, because she was blessed with natural beauty, but she still dressed in a way that would command attention everywhere we went. I guess she felt she needed it.

Despite the coast being Queensland's jewel in the crown, it did lack culture and class. The music scene was limited to a few small pubs that focused on hiring hard rock bands, attracting the rowdy, hard-drinking, head-banging types. That didn't suit me at all.

Natalie introduced me to the only other option we had to expel some of our youthful energy: deafening, seizure-inducing, overcrowded, thumping nightclubs. They filled both sides of one single street in Surfers Paradise and it was in them that I ended up wasting some of the best years of my youth.

What am I doing here? I often questioned why I put myself through it. The choking cigarette smoke, the drunken behaviour, the disorientating, ear-bleeding noise, the confusion and incoherent babble . . . I didn't belong with any of it.

My friends and I were continually sexually harassed from over-sexed males grabbing our behinds and groping our breasts. When we would brave the dance floor, young men continually invaded our personal space and put the moves on us. Sleazy males weren't the only thing we had to contend with. Our poor feet were constantly under attack and being speared by high heels, and our outfits were often soaked in spilled alcohol. Our hair and clothes would stink, and our feet were permanently battered and bruised.

I preferred a much quieter setting where I could actually hear myself think. I longed for stimulating conversations about life and travel, perhaps while sitting at the water's edge, observing the stars and watching the magnificent moonlight lighting up the Pacific Ocean. Give me a campfire and a guitar, and I am at peace.

One evening around eleven o'clock, elbowing my way back from the ladies' bathroom at one club, I was tapped on the shoulder. I turned and instantly recognized the young man who tapped me. I was not thrilled to see this guy one bit.

* * *

When I first moved to the coast and was still dating my first boyfriend Mitchell, this bloke was a friend of his flatmate. Despite his good looks, this blonde-haired, eighteen-year-old kid spoke with so many vulgar obscenities that it astonished me. His mouth was one of the worst I had ever encountered. When he spoke, he would make extremely repugnant comments, honestly making him sound like a rapist.

"Yeah, I got this chick's number, and now I can't wait to knock her down and fuck her stupid," he remarked on one occasion. "I reckon she needs to get my hard cock right uppa!" he added.

I never felt easy around him. I tried telling Mitchell that I thought he was bad news, but he largely ignored me, being more concerned about trying to make friends I guess. It disappointed me hugely that he excused his behaviour so flippantly.

One afternoon, I was simply unable to take any more vulgarity from that vile jerk, so I decided to leave. I was almost out the door, but Mitchell, unaware of the danger he was putting me in, suggested his friend go with me.

"You can double Joy on ya bike, can't ya mate?" he proposed. I shot him a death look that he ignored.

"Yeah, right'o," he grinned.

An ominous feeling of dread came over me, as if I were about to board the Titanic.

"No, I'll be fine by myself," I argued.

"No, I don't wantcha walking home by yourself," Mitchell said adamantly, giving me no choice in the matter.

Reluctantly, I lifted my leg over the frame of his speedster, arranging myself behind him on the parcel rack and grabbing the metal frame rather than holding onto him. I was attempting to erect an invisible barrier between us, not wanting to touch him in any way. He started peddling, and we took off up the street. After riding up just one block, filth started spewing forth from his mouth.

"So, waddaya reckon if I sucked on those nice titties of yours?" he impudently stated. "You look like ya need a good hard fuck too!" To add to my mortification, he reached his hand behind him and grabbed at my crotch. "You couldn't be satisfied with that loser you're with surely. You need someone like me to give it to ya rough like I reckon."

"Just let me off here!" I cried out in cold panic. I was completely disgusted and needed to get away from him urgently. My house wasn't that far away, and I didn't want him knowing where I lived. He brought his bicycle to a slow stop at the next corner.

As I dismounted, he grabbed at my breasts and then my crotch. "Oh you're not going, are ya? Come on, baby, dontcha want my fat cock? You can suck my balls too if ya want!" he offered.

"No thanks, bye!" I blurted, unable to think of a better response. My feet darted across the footpath so quickly that I made it home in less than five minutes.

After arriving through the door, I slipped up the hall and shot into my bedroom. The moment I sat on my bed, hot tears streamed down my face. *Why didn't Mitchell listen to me? How did he not see that was going to happen? What am I supposed to do? Do I tell Mitchell what he just did, or should I not even bother? He probably wouldn't even care.* I wasn't sure about anything anymore.

While struggling to breathe through the raw intensity of having just been violated, I scanned over my short life, trying to find anything that could help me process what was the appropriate thing to do. *Am I overreacting? Are girls supposed to be okay with this type of behaviour?* I thought about my sister.

* * *

I was ten years old and standing in line at a takeout hamburger shop with my older sister, Kerry, who was then sixteen. She was in front of me in the line, and two young guys of similar age were checking her out and nudging each other. The tall one pinched her backside. She immediately whipped around, her eyes darting to find the culprit. The guilty one fessed up by smiling smugly and shrugging his shoulders as if to say, "Well you're pretty, so what do you expect!"

I was waiting for her to tell him off or to at least frown at him, but she astounded me with no response whatsoever. She even returned his smile and faced back to the counter, maintaining the ladylike manners that Mum had taught us girls to display at all times.

The flawed lesson I learned that day was that girls subjected to unwanted male attention were not to react badly, only to smile and largely ignore what was being done to them, even if was an injustice to their gender. If my sister, who was older and wiser, didn't react, then I figured I wasn't supposed to react to what that wanker had just done to me on the bicycle, right?

I felt I didn't have much choice about the matter. I decided to remain silent and just absorb the atrocious infringement upon my being.

Shortly after that incident, Mitchell's flatmate moved out. I felt such relief that I never had to see that lecherous creep again, that was until now, because here he was standing right in front of me in the club.

* * *

"G'day!" he greeted smugly, expectant of my full attention. "Remember me?" he asked.

I offered him no more of me than a simple nod and planned to keep walking, but he stopped me by grabbing my arm.

"So are you here with that Mitchell guy?" he asked abruptly.

"No, we broke up ages ago," I foolishly answered. *Stupid, stupid!*

At that moment, his hand wrapped around my wrist, and I was immediately being led through the crowd. His grip was firm, and his tug was commanding, preventing me from any kind of escape. He reefed me towards the front doors, causing me to almost trip along the way.

"Where are you taking me?" I asked, shouting to be heard over the music.

"You're comin' with me. I got somethin' to show ya!" He wouldn't say anything more, but by the speed at which I was being tugged, I irrationally thought it must have been a matter of supreme importance.

Once outside the front doors, I was led through the parking lot. We scurried through an assortment of cars in what seemed to be a very big hurry.

"What's going on?" I begged with growing impatience.

"Just wanna show ya somethin'." He remained mysterious, unwilling to explain.

We stopped at a beat-up, old white sedan that was covered in dirt and rust. He shuffled around in the front pockets of his jeans and removed some keys. He unlocked the front door, opened it and reached in and unlatched the back door as well. He then climbed into the back seat, while I naively assumed he was about to get this "important" thing he wanted to show me. Instead of leaving, I just foolishly stood there waiting. It was a mighty pull that hurtled me into the back seat with him, which shocked me and jarred my shoulder.

"Come 'ere. It's in 'ere," he lied.

It all happened so quickly. One moment I was inside a club with my friends and the next I was being dragged into a back seat with a guy who had previously assaulted me, and he had just shut the door on us! If I had known what was about to take place, I would have done everything in my power to get away beforehand. I didn't think anyone would be brave enough to attempt what he was about to do, right out there in the open, in full view of anyone coming or going, but I was mistaken.

No sooner did he close the door, than he pounced on me like a ravenous panther. He came in strong with his bourbon-soaked mouth, pressing his lips hard onto mine, then ramming his revolting tongue deep into my throat. I gagged. His calloused hands grabbed at my breasts, squeezing and pinching them hard, causing a tremendous shooting pain to travel from my nipples to my throat. His fingers then tugged at the buttons on my shirt, yanking them, busting my top open and exposing my bra. He ripped at that as well, tearing it so my breasts became uncovered.

Terror overcame me like I had never experienced before. I tried to fight against him. His strength overpowered me.

He wanted my skirt next. It was long to my ankles, so it took him a few attempts to bunch up all the material and get to my underpants. While he was struggling with all of the cloth, I jabbed him with my heels and punched his body with my fists. He wasn't moved or stopped. He clutched at my underpants, scratching my thighs in the process, jerking them down hard. I wriggled to try to get some distance between us, pushing against him. His determination was unrelenting.

An even deeper terror came over me, realizing how hopelessly trapped I felt. I was completely incapable of eyeing any escape. I knew at that moment I was about to be raped, yet I was defenseless, unable to do one damn thing about saving myself from this impending assault.

He unzipped his jeans and shoved his dick inside me. I resisted his revolting invasion, pushing, pinching, scratching, but nothing interrupted his merciless mission. I sucked in air to scream. He slapped his hand over my mouth, silencing me. My lips were ground into my teeth. He thrust himself inside me. I was pinned underneath him, unable to move and barely able to breathe.

I felt suddenly severed from the world. My body may have been in this time and place, but in my despair, I let my mind step into another dimension. I sensed a strange connection to those who had told of their miraculous survival stories. I recalled hearing their accounts about how they became trapped under a rock or a fallen tree branch and were powerless of do anything, being at the mercy of whatever was going to happen to them. I understood what that felt like for a few long moments. I was the one trapped under something, and it was a filthy, vile piece of shit who gave me no choice but to just endure whatever the low-life scumbag decided he wanted to do with *my* body. I couldn't even grit my teeth, as his hands were pushing my lips down so hard into them. I went numb, squeezing my eyes tight, thinking that it would soon be over.

It finally was. He was finished with me.

"Aah, that's better. I feel really good now!" he exclaimed without an ounce of compunction. He then rose and straightened himself up, buckling his belt, smirking at me with his piercing green eyes, letting me know he was pleased. After composing himself, he took one last look in the rear-view mirror then opened the car door, climbing out, leaving me there to "fix myself up."

Did he just say that he feels "good" now?

My blood boiled in my veins. I started feeling the friction burns from where his hands had pushed down on my mouth. The place on my hip where the seatbelt had been sticking me, and the insides of my thighs, the soft places on my body that he'd grabbed at and scratched were all stinging.

The whole ordeal took place in less than five minutes. I swallowed hard, parched and in desperate need of water. I had to get back inside, my friends would be frantically searching for me, and I needed to get back so we could get the hell away from there.

When I re-entered the club, I spotted my rapist over beside the bar with his newly ordered drink. I kept to the other side of the room, barely glancing in his direction. He raised his glass to me with a smug, arrogant grin.

I found my friends and explained that I wanted to go. One of my friends, Karen, could see my distress and decided to take me home. I filled her in on what had happened along the way. To my horror, she admitted that she had experienced similar situations, and not just once, but a number of times.

She'd had guys, quite a few of them, violate her in similar ways, a few in parking lots, some inside the club in the men's room, some at their place, some at hers. She spoke as if it was just part and parcel of being young, female and going out to clubs and being around guys.

"Yeah, I've already had heaps of guys that asked me to go outside with them. I used to go with them only really expecting a kiss or a snuggle or something, but nah, they always had to go all the way!" she stated factually. She added that one even pulled out and came in her hair, then kicked her out of his car for looking too messed up.

When I questioned her further about it, she went on to say that almost all of her sexual encounters were quick, meaningless, mostly forced acts that left her to find her own way home afterwards. She shrugged her shoulders. "Oh well, boys are always horny and can't really help themselves I suppose," she said, brushing off her assaults as if she had to pay the price of being attractive. "It's just what boys do!"

Her attitude both shocked and horrified me. That just didn't seem right. *How could she excuse that so easily? Is she just going to accept that males can't help themselves from raping someone?* Hearing her acquiescence didn't do me any good. It taught me the worst possible lesson of my life and completely led me down the wrong path. She urged me to just accept it and let it go.

"You'll be okay. Just be a bit more aware next time."

Was she serious? Did I really have to accept the insulting and desecrating act of being physically and emotionally raped just like that?

According to my friend, apparently I did.

Chapter 7

My mother could absorb pain like no other. Despite the agony the Multiple Sclerosis caused her, it was imperceptible through her permanent cheerful smile and loving, outstretched arms. Unless you caught her flinching when she thought nobody was watching, you wouldn't know the amount of pain she truly suffered. She hid it all behind her hand-patting, forehead-kissing, benevolent soul.

I attempted to emulate her positive attitude, trying the same optimistic approach to cope with my unexpressed pain and suffering that lingered from the night I crossed over to the other side of rape. If she could deal with her anguish and agony, then so could I. Whenever I felt disturbing cries rising up from within, I would simply deflect them away with a smile. As the victimized part of me would start to slip silently into an all-encompassing torment, the resilient part of me would attempt to shrug it off. I smiled and tried to focus on a bright future, still full of opportunities and prospects. I wanted to be the happy daughter that my parents could be proud of, the person my mother was—positive, smiling and always moving forward.

Over the weeks and months, cracks slowly started appearing on my shell, and I struggled to maintain my façade. Whenever my siblings would criticize me, tease me, snicker or laugh at my every move or decision, it would wound me more deeply. When I desperately needed comfort and support, all I seemed to receive was disapproval and put-downs.

Adolescence was hard enough on its own, yet I was trying to cope with having been sexually assaulted, as well as with constant harassment from men out in the world and endless hurtful insensitivities from my siblings. On top of that, I was expected to continually placate my recovering alcoholic father whenever he had one of his explosive mood swings. It all twisted into a constricted knot of torture and would result in sudden outbursts and tears. The resilient part of me wasn't managing, and it was difficult finding a reason to keep going.

I struggled trying to use Mum's coping mechanisms. Positivity is a wonderful thing, and I desperately wanted to harness its energy like she could, but faking happiness just seemed to trivialize the impact of what happened to me. I had to get real. There was an intense, blood-boiling rage inside me, and there was no shade of white bright enough to erase it.

Over the next few months, I began losing a considerable amount of weight, yet nobody showed even the slightest bit of concern. My family only teased me about it, calling me "Anna the Anorexic" and assuming I was moody, hormonal or retarded.

Despite me wanting to share a close bond with my siblings, it just never happened. I tried many times to confide in them but they would routinely cut me off mid-sentence to ram their advice down my throat, instead of just listening and being supportive. I feared telling them because of their inappropriate and cold reactions. I had no one to turn to.

Mum could never cope with bad news at all. You could only approach her with smaller problems, and she would lovingly pat your hand and offer you a cup of tea to dissolve your blues away. The news of her daughter being raped would have overloaded her. She had enough of her own pain to deal with, and I didn't think she could cope with mine too. Nobody could have offered me the level of support and comfort I really needed. If I had told Dad, he would have just tried to kill the guy. It wasn't exactly comforting to imagine him flying into a rage, and it only made me more afraid to say anything to him. None of my friends were the right people to turn to either. They had their own similar experiences and didn't know how to deal with it correctly. Their answer was to remain in denial and to just accept the rape culture as the social norm. They believed there was nothing they could do about it, even if they wanted to.

The more I kept silent, the more I needed help. All I longed for was to have someone hug me. I mean really squeeze me so hard that all of the burning fury inside me would spew forth like a volcano and leave my body forever. I also needed professional counselling, but it simply didn't occur to me. I felt I had no choice but to tough it out on my own.

* * *

One day, out of absolutely nowhere, a feeling of horrendous dread came crashing down upon me like an avalanche. It was so powerful that I panicked. Paralysed by such frightful anxiety, I couldn't breathe. My heart pounded like a jackhammer. I had no control over this unrelenting force. The room tipped and spun, and I was seized with the unmitigated, terrifying belief that I was about to die. The otherwise clear and reasonable workings of my mind became suddenly impossible to negotiate with.

After about a minute of enduring the cyclonic intensity of this experience, I gradually emerged from its grip, a smoking ruin of bewilderment. I didn't understand it, nor could I even begin to explain it. All I knew was that it was very real, and it left behind a torturous fear of a repeat attack.

And it did repeat, a week later. Another came a few days after that, and then they started happening more frequently, until they were almost daily. Then soon they *became* daily, and then more than one daily, until I became an anxiety-filled wreck. This continued on for months.

The utter exhaustion of going through the attacks, trying to understand them and even attempting to control them, was a gargantuan task with absolutely no success. The attacks had no off switch. All I could do was hold on for dear life and attempt to get through them one horrendous moment at a time.

Depression soon followed. Nothing I did made me happy anymore. Not the songbirds in the morning, the sparkling ocean or even my beloved travel plans. It wounded me tremendously that I couldn't feel anything but fear, loneliness and sadness. They had become part of my daily life, and I had nobody to turn to. I felt alienated from all the happy faces of the world. I couldn't seem to find a way to crawl out from under the blackness. My plans for a wonderful, exciting life had all but perished.

Most nights I dreamed of hitting people right in the mouth. Their faces were unfamiliar yet always male. I felt such outrageous wrath towards them that I really wanted to beat them to a pulp. What infuriated me about the dreams was that each time I swung my arm, I would struggle against invisible resistance, as if I were under water, leaving me weak and powerless. It was impossible for me to make any physical connection between my clenched fist and their faces, and the frustration of being defeated every single time left me feeling unfulfilled and angry, having to always surrender to being the victim.

I lost all interest in going out. My flatmate Natalie was now working at one of the nightclubs and was always out partying with her co-workers, leaving me on my own most of the time.

My clothing choices darkened, and I shadowed about wearing mostly black and jeans, subconsciously attempting to protect myself. I had a new job working in hospitality but never felt hospitable, only disconnected and distant. I began to separate from everyone around me. I noticed nice-looking young men, but beneath their shells I could only see an assailant in every one of them.

The anxiety didn't let up, nor did my depression. It was exhausting and draining me in ways I didn't feel I could return from. I had become desperate for an end to it all.

* * *

My plans were set. I worked out how I was going to do it. After dark, I would drive myself into town, find a high-rise with the easiest access to the roof and simply jump off. All I had to do was make that first leap, and it would be all over. I was about seven hours away from chucking it all in.

A higher power must have decided there was a better use for me, because half an hour after making my perilous plans, my sister, Kerry, and brother-in-law, Glen, appeared framed within my doorway.

"We just bought new body boards! Come with us. We're going to the beach now to try them out. Get your stuff!" They bounced.

"Okay, I guess," I agreed. Why not? A final visit to the sand and surf didn't seem to be such a bad idea for my last few hours alive on earth.

I summoned every last vestige of bravery I thought I had lost and arranged myself atop Glen's board, just as he instructed. Leading me out past the first breaks, farther and farther out to where it became deep and potentially dangerous, Glen kept reassuring me I'd be okay. We caught up to a cluster of rubber-suited wave enthusiasts, sitting on boards, worshipping their liquid God, and we all waited patiently.

Now petrified in anticipation of a foaming, lashing wave plunging me headfirst into its turbulence and drowning me, I realized at that very moment that I didn't want to die. *How could I possibly throw myself from a building when all I want to do is save myself from becoming pummelled into a watery oblivion?*

As a large wave started forming in front of me, I gripped the board, tensed my body and held my breath.

"Okay, this one . . . this is a big one, so get ready . . . Okay it's coming now, so turn around . . . Now start paddling . . . Paddle, paddle, paddle . . . Okay, this is it . . . Go, go, go!" Glen shouted.

I kicked my two feet wildly, as if being chased by Jaws himself, while the rising mountain of water boosted me up on its towering summit. I clung to the foam floatation device, propelled forward with a thundering, mighty force. I steered that sucker nervously onward, clutching firmly, balancing myself, putting every flicker of hope and trust into the big cheese upstairs that he would let me make it back to shore. A burst of crazy exhilaration erupted deep within me and electro-charged my every cell. I felt so alive! I clung on and rode that board all the way into shore, triumphantly!

It was the most vitalizing thrilling, adrenalin-charged one-minute ride of my life. Even when the board slowed to a dead stop upon the wet sand, I continued to lie on top, clinging to its sides. I wished my magnified, tingling goosebumps could last for eternity.

For the first time in months, in years, I felt absolutely overjoyed. My heart, my nervous system, my skin, my electrical impulses had all erupted with euphoria, and not only was I back, I was better than ever! As I lay on that board, puffing and beaming, I had an epiphany. If it only took one minute for God to prove that life is worth living, then that was a heck of a way to do it! If I could get that amount of jubilation from just that *one* thing in life, then how much more did it have to offer? Infinite amounts surely! Oh the things I could look forward to. *Thank you for giving me such a wonderful gift and literally saving my life. Amen.*

My head raced with plans. I not only dropped my drastic and reckless plans of doing away with myself, but also immediately began making new, better, colourful plans. I couldn't wait to start a vision board. I felt invigorated once again about life, travel and adventure. I even had new hope of meeting some lovely guy who shared my passions so we could go on extraordinary journeys together.

Over the subsequent days, weeks and months, I started cutting out pictures from magazines and brochures. Natalie was out clubbing most nights, and more often than not, I stayed home snipping out pictures of all the places I wanted to visit.

I favoured the photos of women who had particular elated expressions. They appeared as I wanted to feel, experiencing something so fantastic that I could imagine my face looking that happy as well. Every picture I found with an experience I wanted for myself, I sheared, sliced, and trimmed neatly and glued it to my board.

With new determination for an adventurous and amazing life, I felt ready to try again. I felt that I could face whatever and whoever was going to obstruct the realization my dreams.

Chapter 8

When it came to looking for a suitable mate to share my life with, the young men that were available were rather lacking in class, sophistication and charm, qualities that would have gone a long way in attracting the interest of a young lass. Basic good manners were nowhere to be found, and there wasn't any proper dating etiquette being followed. They seemed to have no idea how to ask a girl out properly or see them home in a gentlemanly custom. Many of our boys would simply unzip their pants with misguided expectation at the end of a date.

They assumed they could turn a girl's head by proudly bragging about how "smashed" they got on the weekend, or how they were arrested for doing a "legendary" burnout. Hardly any of them seemed at all interested in talking about travel, art, nature, history or the wonders of the universe. Instead, the only conversation they were interested in having was either about porn, criminal behaviour, drinking excessively, screaming music, getting wasted and hooning around in their cars.

To be considered a real man in our culture, you had to at least, if nothing else, be a hoon. A *hoon* is typically someone who drives recklessly, screeches and smokes up their tires, skids and speeds, performs hazardous burnouts, usually in muscle cars, and acts like a complete idiot, putting everybody's lives in extreme danger.

To gain an even higher rank was to reach a true bogan status. A *bogan* is someone who takes pride in being rough around the edges, with their clothing, attitude and behaviour exemplifying an anti-authoritarian stance. You cannot be a bogan without also being a hoon, and you need to drink to excess, have home-done tattoos and a love of all things course, vulgar and loud. Bogan guys would slop around in sleeveless flannelette shirts, work shorts and flip-flops (which we call *thongs*), with most having bad teeth and very poor hygiene.

Excessive drinking was, and still is, our greatest national pastime. Any excuse, anytime, anywhere and with whoever will drink. Young men my age couldn't wait to shoot off down to the pub and start binge drinking until they became thoroughly intoxicated. That's when they started acting like real idiots. Australia Day, Christmas, Easter, none of our holidays were celebrated with the honour and respect they deserved. Instead they were just an excuse to party hard and get as wasted as they possibly could.

It's not that I had anything against them all. Far from it. Many possessed a certain cheeky quality I enjoyed (affectionately known as *larrikins)* and generally, Australian men were down-to-earth, friendly and attractive blokes. Having said that, the only ones who appeared available at the time were Ned Kelly idolizers or *dole bludgers*. Those guys appeared to be quite proud of being unemployed bums, because they bragged about spending three to six hours every day catching "killer" waves.

The tradies that were around looked okay but it was the culture and attitude surrounding their occupation that was a major turn off. They were widely known for being the worst offenders of sexual harassment. Their whistling, catcalling, hooting and hollering would rain down at every female who dared to walk by them. Their general sexist, lewd and crude behaviour was gaining international attention, and they had earned themselves quite the reputation. It seemed that every male *brickie*, *chippie* and *sparkie* (or for non-Australians: bricklayer, carpenter and electrician) acted as if he was entitled to behave that way, as an entitlement of his chosen career.

Many asked me out, but I started to turn them down after one of them, a mechanic, got so drunk on our date that for most of the night, he was passed out in the bushes. Afterwards, I ended up having to drive us both home, and he threw up on me in the car on the way.

Natalie dated a lot of guys, but none that were the type that would ever stick around. I never interfered with her fun, but I just couldn't see the appeal in all those brief and meaningless encounters. The minute those guys got what they wanted, they disappeared. False promises, fake charm, lies, deception—anything they could use to lure a female into their beds—they would use it. Once they conquered their female prey, they were history. Natalie said she wasn't bothered by it, but I could tell she was lying.

I was honest with myself and knew I couldn't develop that carefree, one-night-stand mentality. I wanted a real relationship with someone on the same page as I was. It would have been a bonus to be protected from all those foul-mouthed blokes out there and from further dates from hell. I didn't need to get married straight away, and I certainly had no desire to start a family anytime soon, that's why I had let Mitchell go. I may have regretted that decision. At least he didn't cheat on me. He was a better guy than Mikey and far better than anyone on the Gold Coast that I'd seen.

* * *

I had heard on the grapevine that Mikey's baby had arrived. Apparently his new girlfriend had given birth to a boy a few weeks earlier, and they were both living together next door to his parent's house near Surfers Paradise. I thought I would try to be an adult about what had happened and pay them a visit to offer my congratulations. It just felt right to show them that I had no hard feelings. To this day, I still don't know why I felt obliged to do that. Not only was it unnecessary, but it was also just plain stupid. As it turned out, it ended up being one of the worst decisions I ever made.

It was a stifling summer's day, and just from the brief ten-minute drive there, the radiator of my rusty heap of junk was pissed with me and starting to overheat. I walked up to the front door and knocked, but nobody responded.

"They aren't home!" Mikey's father called out. He had appeared from the rear side entrance of the house next door.

"Oh hi, I just came to see the baby," I replied gaily.

"They're not there, but come over and say hello," he hollered, waving me over. Mikey's dad was a rotund man, mid-seventies, who sweated profusely and always smelled like garlic. In the extreme heat that day, I took my chances that he might just offer me a cold glass of lemonade. It did seem odd, though, that he asked me to climb over the side fence, rather than simply letting me in through the front door.

With the clumsiness of a green cadet in a *Police Academy* movie, I awkwardly scrambled up and over the wooden hurdle.

"Well done!" he praised. "It's so good to see you!" he greeted, pulling me in for tight squeeze. He grabbed my hand and started leading me towards the side door.

Gee, this is all a bit much, especially just for a cold drink and a quick hello!

He hugged me again when I entered the house. While still squeezing my hand, he led me up the hall towards the living room. I was looking for his wife, who I assumed was home and perhaps in one of the rooms, but when I didn't see her anywhere, I felt confused as to what I was even doing there.

If he is here all alone, then why would he want me to visit him? It's not as if we were ever close. We barely even talked while I dated his son.

Instead of fetching me my drink, he led me over to a grey vinyl sofa, a terrible choice for hot climates as you have to peel yourself off every time you get up. He plopped himself down on the couch and pulled me with him. I clumsily fell beside him. I corrected my posture and arranged myself into a more ladylike position, attempting to regain my dignity. I was still wondering when I'd be getting my lemonade.

Still having a grip on my hand, he then reached his free arm around my shoulder and cuddled me in close to his chest. The stench from his perspiration was suffocating and the wiry hairs poking out from the top of his shirt irritated the skin of my cheek. I almost threw up.

"It's so good to see you!" he repeated with affection. It alarmed me. He had never shown me this much fondness, ever. I attempted to push myself away from his firm embrace, trying to put some distance between us, but he struggled against my efforts to get away, keeping a tight grip upon my shoulder.

Finally letting go of my hand, a fleeting moment of hope that he was finished "greeting" me quickly disappeared as he brought that arm around in front of me, enveloping me in an all-encompassing, even tighter squeeze.

His sweaty hand then started wandering. I knew at that point that I wasn't there for a quick sociable visit. He began rubbing the right side of my body. I stiffened. His face moved in closer, and my heart started pounding heavily.

His hard, aged lips puckered onto my cheek, and he whispered in my ear, "It's so good you are here."

A blend of garlic and strong coffee on his breath overpowered my senses, causing me to turn away. I was reeling from the odour. He continued rubbing his wandering hand up and down along the right side of my body. My heart thumped harder. When he started sliding his hand around to my front, my breath stalled. I became almost paralysed from the intensity of my new terror. He then slid his hand down onto my right breast. A cold panic rose up within me with such force that I burst out of his hold, breaking free and shooting straight to my feet.

"What are you doing?" I brashly demanded. I wasn't thinking, only reacting, from shock, disgust and confusion. I was actually quite proud of myself for doing *that* much.

"Nothing, I'm not doing nothing," he claimed, shrugging his shoulders. He showed me his empty hands as if feigning innocence, offering me nothing more than a blameless expression as he sat there looking pathetic.

I was at a complete loss as to what to do. *Do I yell at this guy, or do I have to still show him respect as my ex-boyfriend's father? Do I treat this as nothing, like he is desperately trying to do, or am I supposed to cause a scene?*

"Oh okay, you worried me there for a moment," I said, letting him off the hook, being disappointed with my response. Showing respect to the parents of your friends, or to any adult for that matter, was foremost in my thoughts, but I still had to get out of there. "Okay, got to go, bye!" I rattled nervously, leaping towards the door. "And if you see Mikey, tell him hello and congratulations on the baby." *God I'm such an idiot!*

I scurried outside and climbed back into my overheated crap heap, trembling as if it were only six degrees outside instead of thirty-six. I started the engine and took off in a blind panic. No more than one block away, my old piece of junk started spewing steam from under the hood, and the temperature gauge had reached its limit. I could see up ahead that the main road was heavily congested, so I decided to pull over. I could walk to my parent's apartment from there. *Maybe Dad can drive me back later with some water for the radiator.*

That next thirty-minute walk was torturous. I was still trembling and sickened from that ordeal, and now I was sweltering from the sun as it relentlessly beat down upon me. It seared my unprotected skin, causing it to sting as if I had been attacked by a thousand bees. With every sun-scorched step I took, I became increasingly angry, not only with my defective, broken-down piece of junk, but with that dirty old bastard. *I can't believe my ex-boyfriend's father, who is three times my age, someone who I thought I could trust, tried to put his filthy mouth on me. Who the hell does he think he is, having the audacity to rub his dirty mits all over my body? If I had not gotten away when I did, goodness knows what he was going to do to me. As if I would ever be interested in that sweaty, old pervert anyway. Fucking creep!*

The intensity of the heat and stress of the day was beginning to overwhelm me. I was completely parched and really quite faint. I could feel myself starting to sway, feeling the temptation to surrender to the heaviness and just black out, but I needed to hold on. I was walking along the main road into town, and I would be helpless and humiliated if I dropped where I was.

Just then, a car blasted its horn at me. "Come on baby, show us your tits!" a group of young blokes called out.

It jerked me to sobering attention and rattled me even deeper. I trudged on. A few minutes later another car did the same exact thing.

"Oh yeah, baby, nice ass!" They whistled and tooted as they drove on by, completely oblivious how fucked up that was.

Hot tears were welling up, but I promptly blinked them back. Two more cars tooted and more male voices called out. I became so furious and overcome by the heat, I was only seconds from passing out.

I arrived on my parent's doorstep just in time. I turned up burnt, dehydrated, faint, furious and shaken. The second I sat down on their sofa, tears flooded my eyes and spilled forth.

"What's the matter, darling?" Mum asked, worried.

I blurted out what had happened.

Dad, who had been standing close by in the kitchen, upon hearing me say who it was, disappeared in a flash.

Mum soothed me with one of her loving pats on the hand. "There, there, darling, now let's try to not let that stupid man upset you. Why don't you go wash your face, and then you can make us a nice cup of tea," she softly suggested. Having to ask me to make the tea would have been difficult for her, because if there was ever a time that she would want to physically do something for any of her children, that would have been one of them.

She clicked her remote control unit at the TV until stopping on an old Fred Astaire movie. "Come on. Let's watch this. This is one of our favourites. It should take your mind off all that rubbish," Mum proposed, reducing me to a reluctant speechlessness.

I stared at the screen but couldn't focus. For the first time, Fred's effortless, flawless moves weren't capturing my attention. I was too disturbed, too violated.

Dad returned thirty minutes later. Mum and I glared quizzically at him, waiting for an explanation to his disappearance.

"Don't worry about him anymore, Midget. He shouldn't bother you again," he offered without elaboration.

Mum and I both understood what he meant. He had obviously been over there and confronted Mikey's dad.

My father's intervention on my behalf was appreciated, but did not leave me with the satisfaction of personally giving him a piece of mind. What I really needed was my own version of closure, but I didn't know how to go about it. I never got the chance, nor did I really have the courage to confront these males, and every time someone else messed with me, even in the slightest way, old wounds that were still raw would erupt in volcanoes of anger and anguish.

So much for my new attitude. I now had to come to terms with the fact that I was permanently damaged, and no cup of tea, positive attitude or vision board would make it all go away.

Chapter 9

The moments when I would catch my own reflection, I often wondered what people saw. I never considered myself all that attractive. There were a couple of things I suppose were satisfactory, my overall shape and perhaps my eyes, but I didn't think my face or general appearance was anything special. In fact, there were many parts of me that would cause me to cringe.

I hated my hair and still do. My natural shade of strawberry blonde was the subject of endless taunts and name calling at school. It made me loathe it early on. Redheads have always had a rough time in Australia, for reasons that I still cannot understand. It ultimately led to the ruination of my self-esteem. The moment I turned eighteen, I started trying to bleach all the red out. I wasn't aware back then that blondes attracted more male attention. I learned *that* lesson the hard way. It seemed as though I was damned if I was a blonde *or* a redhead.

Another part I didn't like about my appearance was my smile. It turned my eyes into slits and gave me creases and lines on my face that I wasn't ready for. I always thought it made me look awful. My skin was far too sensitive for the sunny state of Queensland, and I developed major sun damage over the years, resulting in red, scaly solar spots all over my arms and legs that I can never hide. Besides my flaming hair, crinkly smile and sensitive skin, I also thought my chest was too small, my lips were too thin, and I never liked my nose or my natural speaking voice.

Every female tends to scrutinize herself far too much, and I was no different that way. That said, I largely accepted what I was given and didn't obsess or fuss with myself too much. I never spent more than half an hour getting ready to go anywhere, and however I put myself together, I was somewhat content with the result. I was a long way from being beautiful, a very long way, but I was at least presentable.

Whatever I *may* have had going for me, it certainly garnered me way too much attention—the wrong kind of attention. The only upside to not being totally repulsive was that I was regularly presented with males who asked me out.

I met one young man, Martin, at a party, and for the first time, I became involved in an unexpectedly stimulating conversation. We spoke about travel and life and nature, and what was even more unexpected, he was surprisingly well-spoken and pleasantly well-mannered. I liked that he was an artist, because creative people are usually more in touch with their spiritual side. I enjoyed hearing his stories about his European trip, which enthralled me for hours.

He was not muscular or tan like a lot of the local boys. This fellow was tall and lean with a likeable face. Physical appearances were never my focus anyway. I only ever wanted to be with a good-natured, kind and courteous person who displayed good manners and had a great sense of fun. Martin ticked all those boxes. At first anyway.

We started seeing each other over the following weeks, developing a relationship, and we became a couple. I had high hopes that he was the guy I had been dreaming about.

Over the months, the long commute on the bus to see him at his flat on the far end of the coast became wearisome. Given that he made no effort to visit me, we decided it was logical to have me move in with him and his flatmate. If nothing else, it was a matter of convenience.

It was amazing just how quickly the glossy patina wore off my new boyfriend after I'd unpacked my bags and I was no longer enamoured. Now that I was around him all the time, he couldn't hide his habits. He was without question an addicted dope smoker, and so were all his mates. More often than not, he and his buddies would all sit around, get high and talk nonsense. When that happened, I would retreat into our bedroom and shut the door. The second-hand dope smoke made me choke, and I became dizzy and sick. When his mates weren't there, he would get stoned by himself. Either way, he couldn't go very long without having it in his system.

Martin turned out to be a great disappointment. He wasn't anything like he had led me to believe. I had hoped he was the one I could have new adventures with, the guy who would get just as excited about packing our bags and looking at maps. But it seemed the only thing that excited him was smoking dope and watching porn. He loved to watch it every night after I had gone to bed, something I discovered one night when I got up for a glass of water and caught him watching it.

"Well if a man doesn't get his quota!" his excuse was.

What quota? This is the first I've heard about some sexual expectancy that he apparently has? Now I'm made to feel like I'm not fulfilling his needs. How is that fair? I didn't even know about them.

Martin wasn't like Mikey. He didn't ask anything of me sexually that I was uncomfortable with. In fact, he was kind of a dud in the bedroom, and we barely did anything, but I was okay with that. So I was really quite shocked to find out he had been watching all this porn but never followed up on anything he must have been *learning*. I had never seen porn before then—I mean the kind that involved actual people and not animals—and from the couple of seconds that I glimpsed, I thought it looked quite disgusting. He never told me he had any porn, never once even mentioned it, so it upset me that he had kept it from me and then blamed me for being upset when I discovered he had been keeping secrets. Men and their secrets and lies really put a bee in my bonnet, but I let it go. It took me decades to realize, however, that it wasn't about me. I carried that around with me for way too long and always felt that I was never enough.

At a small gathering of a few people, Martin admitted that he was at a *dare party* just before he met me, where one of his buddies was dared to go into the back bedroom and "do the deed" with his girlfriend. Unbeknownst to this couple, all of his mates crept down the side of the house and watched the two of them going at it from outside the bedroom window. Naturally that shocked and horrified me. *What a disgraceful breach of privacy! Is every male a dirty voyeur who watches people through windows? If they had done that to me, I would have chopped every single one of their peckers off with an axe and had a murder of crows gouge their eyes out!*

One afternoon, after Martin and I had just returned from the beach, about five of his mates arrived. They quickly became comfortable, turning on the TV and cracking open a few beers. There was a cheesy teenage movie playing, and a scene involving a wet T-shirt competition had soon captivated them all. They hooted and cheered while I was in the kitchenette behind them, trying to make lunch. I wasn't given much of a chance to change out of my swimming costume before they all suddenly appeared, but I had at least thrown on a large white T-shirt overtop.

The packet of bread that I was holding was suddenly ripped from my hands, and the next thing I knew, I was being thrown down onto the kitchen table. Four of them had sprung from their chairs and pounced on me, pinning my ankles and wrists in place. I couldn't move. They cackled and snickered as they held me down. I was petrified!

I tried wriggling and kicking my way free, but they held me down forcefully. Martin then grabbed the pitcher of water I had just prepared moments earlier and poured the entire contents over me, emptying it all over my chest, thoroughly soaking my T-shirt and my swimmers underneath.

The room erupted with a joint chorus of "Woohoo, nice titties! Here's our wet T-shirt winner!" They were whooping and shouting, some jabbing Martin in his side saying, "Oh, lucky guy, getting to play with those every day!"

I was completely terror struck. They could all see everything. The water had soaked through all that I had on, and my breasts were showing completely through. I struggled and yelled out, "Let me up!" I can still remember the anger I felt at being so violated in that way.

They decided they'd had their fun with me, and it was time to finally let me go. As I scrambled to cover myself, they teased, "What's the matter? They're only boobs. Everyone's got 'em!" When they saw my flushed faced and eyes swelling with ferocious tears, their only recompense was, "Oh don't be so upset. They're only boobs!"

What did I ever do to deserve this, you bunch of dope-headed wankers? I wanted desperately to scream at them, but I was outnumbered. I was up against too many alpha males, and my rage would have been a waste of my energy. I dashed up the hall and hid in the bathroom.

As I wrapped myself in a dry towel, shaking and attempting to breathe deeply and control my fury, I could hear them all leaving. I heard them muttering something about the pub and playing a few rounds of pool. "See you soon, Marty, we'll save you a beer?"

I was more pissed off with my boyfriend than any of the other boys, he being the worst offender of all. *How dare he pour that water on me, exposing my body to all his mates and allowing them to taunt me in that way.*

I heard his footsteps plodding up the hall then a soft knock on the bathroom door.

"You okay in there, honey bunch?"

"Go away!" I snapped angrily.

"But . . ."

"No. Piss off, Martin. Just go with your mates and leave me alone." I wasn't ready to forgive anyone just yet.

There was only one other female living in the apartment building. After I changed into some dry clothes, I went and knocked on her door in the hope of some much-needed comfort and female support.

I had gotten to know this lady a little while living in the building. She was around thirty and studying to become a counsellor. I hoped she could offer me some advice. I needed her expertise on how one copes with being victimized, if she knew anything about that. I considered her more of a friend and neighbour than a counsellor, but either way, any listening ear would have been helpful at that point.

She was happy to see me and invited me in. I was offered a seat at the kitchen table where she had been studying. “It looks like something has upset you?”

It was difficult to open up to anyone. I had tried and failed many times before, so it took a bit of prompting from her to get me going.

“If you need to talk, I’m right here,” she offered gently. She could see from my puffy eyes that I needed to unload, and it was good of her to let me interrupt her day.

I started talking about what had just happened and about how it actually scared me how angry it made me. I went on to say how I hated males always sexually harassing me and touching me against my will. I told her about being groped on the bus, in crowded places, or at a club. I explained that it made me furious how I was always being inappropriately spoken to or whistled at out on the street. I didn’t tell her of my rape. I couldn’t. It was just too humiliating. In hindsight, telling someone was the one thing I *should* have done.

She listened and smiled, and I was grateful for that, but I’m not sure if it was her inexperience as a student or because she wasn’t getting paid, but all she really gave me was some empty, impractical advice. “Don’t let those stupid men get to you,” she said. “You are better than that, stronger than that, and you just need to ignore them.”

Wow! That’s it? That’s what my mother says! I thought this lady was learning to be a professional. Is that all I am going to get in this life, empty advice that doesn’t help me? Where exactly am I supposed to draw strength from?

I took small comfort in her methods of practice. Either she didn’t want to admit that her course didn’t cover sexual violation, or that it did, but she just sucked at it. That type of advice was not helpful in the least. Trying to treat deep wounds that continued to re-open with shallow, perky pep talks just left me feeling worse. I wasn't exactly sure what I needed to hear, but that wasn't it.

She did, however, follow up with an invitation to go with her and her friend to the beach the following day. I guess an extension of friendship is never a bad thing. I accepted her invitation but felt just as bad when I left her apartment as I had when I entered.

The following day, the three of us met and walked across the road to the beach together. They were both around the same age, about eight years older than me. Her friend, obviously quite comfortable with herself and her body, decided to go topless. Trying to carry on a normal conversation with someone exposing her breasts for all the world to see was about as uncomfortable as seeing your own father naked. There I was, doing my utmost to keep mine protected, and yet I was sitting next to someone perfectly happy to put them on display.

It reminded me of being at the beach with my two sisters and their friends back in Melbourne. I was around twelve years old, and some of them would sunbathe topless. A line-up of guys would constantly approach them. I remember one young man in particular, sauntering up quite boldly to one of the friends and remarking, "Geez, ya got nice tits!"

"Gee, thanks!" she replied, as if being complimented on her hairstyle.

In a way, I envied those girls, how they could just sit on the sand, practically naked, without a care in the world, proudly showing off their puppies. I could never be that free. Men made sure of that. Anywhere I went, I was constantly under threat of attack, even by my own boyfriend.

The three of us settled on the sand. Within less than five minutes, a young boy no more than ten years old appeared and sat down nearby. He began leering at our topless friend. We were aware of his presence but did our best to ignore him. He continued to sit and stare. After a few minutes, he yelled out, "Hey lady, nice tits. Can I suck them?"

I can't believe it! A ten-year-old said that?

"Get out of here, or you'll be in trouble," she called back.

The boy rose up to leave but decided to give one final retort. "Geez lady, I just wanted to suck your tits!" He then took off running.

Oh my, they start so young! Where do they get it in their heads that they can just yell out something like that, especially to adults? Most likely from observing other men I would imagine, their fathers, uncles maybe, older brothers, peers, television. Observing typical Aussie males at their best for sure.

* * *

Occasionally Martin would take me to small gatherings at the homes of his mates, normally low-key affairs, with only a dozen or so people. The girls would band together in the kitchen and chat, while the boys would sit in the lounge, watching porn and getting stoned and drunk.

From what I saw of the pornography playing on the TV, again, it all looked quite disgusting. I wasn't sure what revolted me most, the intimate close-ups of people's most private parts, the vulgar and often warped acts the actors were engaging in, or how Martin's friends all carried on while watching it. They cheered it on voraciously, hooting and hollering, simulating some of the scenes with each other and shouting out vile remarks like, "Yeah, that's it. Give it to her hard!" and "Yeah, yeah, get it up her!" and "Woohoo, cum shot! Yeah, yeah, get it right in her eye!"

I couldn't help but ask them once, "Is this what you guys find amusing?"

The most outspoken one admitted, "Yeah of course, in fact if you weren't here, we'd most likely be jerking off to it right now!"

The thought of such a group activity shocked and horrified me. I mean, seriously, couldn’t they all just play cricket or footy together instead?

A few bragged about how they would deliberately go out wearing loose shorts so they could prop their legs up in a certain way and allow their “misters” to dangle out onto the chair seat. They would proudly show them off, just waiting for the next poor, unsuspecting female victim to notice. They laughed over the fact that most girls couldn’t get away fast enough, and they thoroughly enjoyed watching them being appalled.

That might be slightly funny if they were nine, but these guys are in their twenties! I was aghast at their bold admissions.

After about a year and a half of living with Martin, I had grown tired of waiting for something to change. I had deluded myself that he was as eager to get out into the world as I was. He didn’t seem to want to do much more than smoke pot. If I had stayed in that environment for much longer, I’m sure I would have started slipping under another prolonged eclipse of depression, and I was petrified of revisiting that darkness again. I needed a more beneficial existence and a sounder environment.

It is never easy breaking up with someone, and even though I wasn’t overly smitten with the guy, it was still tough emotionally. Healing is a process, and I still felt alone and really quite sad.

I decided to pop in on Natalie. We hadn’t seen each other much of late, and I didn’t want to lose her friendship. She was always up for spontaneity, so it didn’t surprise me that just after my twenty-fourth birthday, I found myself packing for my first trip overseas with her. We decided we didn’t need boys. We were headed for the South Pacific, just the two of us, on an ocean liner for twelve days of sunbathing, cocktails and the big blue ocean.

“Are we really going to do this?” I nervously asked, waving

my brand-new passport.

"Yes!" she bounced and clapped her hands. "And we are going to have so much fun!"

Is this finally the beginning of the exciting life of travel and adventure I've always dreamed about? I felt a rush of new hope that my life would change in amazing and unexpected ways after all.

Chapter 10

I was bursting at the seams when we departed, jubilantly waving to the cheering crowd below. Thousands of rainbow paper streamers snapped free from the dock as we launched out into the vast blue waters.

I imagined what the islands were going to be like and anticipated interacting with the world's most graceful and brilliantly coloured marine life. I was planning to explore every inch of the magnificent, unspoiled islands of the Pacific.

The *SS Fairstar*, my home for the next twelve days, was not only sailing us away on a wondrous voyage, but it also held a bounty of endless possibilities for shipboard amusement along the way. I placed only the highest of expectations upon the mighty vessel.

After promptly unpacking and fervently scanning over our action-packed schedules, we set out to investigate the ship. I was about as buzzed as one could get, but Natalie thought very little of the movie theatre, the casino, the gym, or the coffee shops. She even sped past the fashion stores with barely a glance. She only seemed interested in one thing, the pool deck. When we finally found our way up there, her eyes widened, and she ardently suggested we spend the rest of the afternoon arranged on some deck chairs.

"Wow!" She beamed with an overextended grin. "Would you look at that? Oh yes, are we going to have ourselves some F–U–N!" She lifted her arms back over her head and posed on her sun lounge like a movie star. Her motivation for cementing herself on her sun-warmed wooden plank became evident after pointing out the smorgasbord of young males that had congregated around us.

Dozens of twenty-something-year-olds, bare-chested and bronzed, began strutting around the deck. Some zealously dived into the large pool in front of us, while others deliberately showed off every muscle they had. Some spread out their towels to get in their first bit of sun-worshipping of the trip. And of course, many had gathered around the bar to blow the froth of their first couple of cold beers, beating their chests and letting out a primitive howl, “Whoooooeeee!”

A quick survey of these early behaviours was enough evidence for me to realize that I was now trapped on a cruise liner with way too many young Aussie blokes on a twelve-day, all-out bender. It wasn’t long before they became half tanked and began approaching us.

Natalie, of course, was in her element, enjoying all the male attention. Being the recipient of their horrid mistreatment over the years, I simply didn’t give a flick about receiving any more of it. I couldn’t have cared less whether I attracted them or not. Despite not being in the mood to be hit on, I remained polite all the same and offered my usual civil, well-mannered pleasantries when they approached, just in case I did meet a real gentleman, however unlikely.

They started by asking the same old questions.

“Where ya from?”

“What d’ya do?”

“Have youse got boyfriends?”

Then it progressed.

“So what’s the kinkiest thing ya done?”

“Have ya ever done it in public?”

“Whatcha doin’ later? Wanna come to my cabin?”

“Ever had a three-way?”

Naturally, there were many bold assumptions we were drug users.

“So d’ya want some smoke?”

“Wanna do some cones with us?”

“What’s ya favourite drug? Are ya into any hard stuff? I can arrange some if you are!”

I would find myself having to go to great lengths to deflect their discourse. I either had to make some excuse to leave, conjure up a fake boyfriend, or invent some illness or some important thing I had to do, which was difficult while wearing a swimming costume. More often than not, I had to somehow drastically change the subject. It was a pressure I hated. Being forced to come up with creative lies and excuses without bruising their fragile egos became exhausting. It was always my stupid fear that kept me from telling them all just to screw off.

Being pushed into retreating was a commonality amongst females that I was discovering more and more. Why did we have to be polite about not wanting to have sex with them? But if we fractured their precious egos in any way, we would be accused of being snobby, pretentious bitches and potentially cause them to retaliate. There was never anything enjoyable, relaxing or reassuring about having conversations with Aussie males. Their egos wouldn't allow it.

I longed to talk to decent young men who could act in a civilized, respectful manner and engage in a genuine, refreshing and inspiring conversation with me without resorting to the skulduggery of trying to get me into bed. If I was lucky enough to encounter that, I was more than happy to get to know them. I ached to be treated with simple appreciation for being an intelligent human being with something to contribute to this world. Sadly, very few seemed able to get past the package I was wrapped in. I was just the girl men disrobed with their eyes and touched without being asked.

In the evenings after dinner and some kind of cabaret show, Natalie would race to get out on deck where the disco would begin nightly at ten o'clock. She would often become deeply entranced with someone around midnight, while I would spend my nights fending off boozy, intrepid wankers slobbering into my hair, mistaking my boobs for my face.

After meeting a few second- and third-time passengers, I soon learned that I was travelling on a ship with a well-known reputation as a guaranteed place to get laid. It didn't surprise me. I also found that I needed to avoid many of the male staff, as they were equally on the prowl. Many of the crew, most whom weren't even Australian, hit on the female passengers, looking for a quick and meaningless romp.

Midmorning on day five, Natalie and I made our way up to the pool deck with our beach towels ready for another day of sunbathing. I was hoping, however, to join in on some fun shipboard activities. I enjoyed just about anything: pool volleyball, table tennis, jogging around the ship, and I was feeling particularly energetic that morning.

Just two minutes after settling into our loungers, before I could spot the activities director, four young guys plopped themselves down beside us. The usual ritual began. They were Sydney boys, and lads from the bigger cities predictably always tried to lure girls by fanning their invisible wads of cash in front of their faces. Their lackluster performance usually failed them. Droning on about fast cars, designer sunglasses and satin sheets wasn't doing it for me. Despite my disinterest, I at least attempted civility and gave the occasional nod and smile. Natalie, however, was lapping up the attention.

I perched my swim bag onto my knee and searched for my tube of sunscreen. After rummaging for over a minute and still coming up empty-handed, I knew I had to walk all the way back to our cabin to fetch it. With my fair skin and constant exposure to the direct sun, I had learned that if I didn't smear that goop on every hour, I would suffer tremendously with a blistering sunburn.

"Natalie, I'm just going to pop down to our cabin for a quick minute. I'll be right back."

She waved me away with a disinterested, "Yeah, yeah bye," while her eyes remained transfixed on the one she obviously thought was cute.

The quietest one of the group, a brown-haired, twenty-something-year-old, immediately shot to his feet. "I'll go with you!" he proclaimed.

My stomach twisted with instant apprehension. *I don't know this guy. I have barely spoken to him. So why would he want to go with me? What kind of ideas would he be having at this hour?* I tried to shoot Natalie an SOS look, but she was so busy feasting her eyes on the tall, dark and handsome one that I lost all hope of being saved. All I could do was try to convince myself that I had nothing to worry about.

He trailed beside me speechlessly as we headed down a maze of corridors. We rode an elevator down three floors, walked through a few more hallways, and then eventually reached my cabin. He barely spoke two words the entire way, which only added to my concern. By the time I had my keys out ready to unlock my door, I was thoroughly convinced he had something more on his mind than just being my chaperone. *What could possibly be in it for him? He obviously isn't here for conversation.*

My gut squirmed as I slipped the key into the lock. I flung the door open wide with a mighty push, and it banged against the wall behind it. I did that deliberately because I wanted anyone who may have been around to be aware of our presence. I ducked in, eyed my tube of sunscreen and snapped it up swiftly.

"Got it!" I leapt back towards the doorway, but he was standing firm in front of it, blocking me with arms that he'd folded like a bouncer at a nightclub.

Acid heat splashed through my veins, and my heart pulsed violently. *Oh no, please no!* I knew at that moment that this young man wanted nothing else but to set upon me. I had to try to keep my fear hidden from him, giving myself one last chance at freedom. I concealed my dread with a smile. "Okay, let's go," I proposed lightly, but he remained a rigid, immovable force.

He placed his left hand against my chest, pushing me backwards, leading us both into the room while flicking the door closed with his right. I was certain he could feel my heart pounding through my chest, and I was angry that it might have given me away.

With both hands, he grabbed my shoulders, pulling me in close to his face. I pushed back. His face came in close again, and he smacked his mouth into my lips, shoving his tongue into my dry, frightened mouth. His "kiss" felt as if a giant slug was frantically trying to burrow deep into my oral cavity. I pushed his chest with my hands, trying to shove him away, but he snickered at my feeble attempt.

He walked me backwards into the room, until I bumped into the bunk bed and reached my impending doom. My breathing turned jagged and shallow as I tried to eye an escape, but I was cornered and completely blocked in by his solid body.

He reached both of his hands around my back, sliding them under my cotton singlet. He pulled the string on my bikini top that I was wearing underneath and loosened it in one fluid motion, giving him now easy access to my chest. His hands slid over me and grabbed at my breasts. I tried prying them off, but he continued to squeeze them. It really hurt.

As I looked up into his eyes, hoping I could reason with him to let me go, all I could see was a vacant lust, almost as if there weren't a person behind them. He had an unyielding determination to conquer my body, and I was of no importance to him. Pleading with him, I could see, was going to be futile.

Effortlessly, he pushed me down onto the bed, and he thumped himself immediately on top, pinning one half of me down and leaving the other half for him to play with. He propped up on his side and started groping me further, moving his hands across my body, rubbing and squeezing my breasts, my stomach and the top of my pubic bone. With soundless tears, I held my breath and tried to hover above myself. He shoved his hand forcefully underneath my shorts, his rough fingers abrasive on my most tender of lady areas.

"Stop!" I pleaded, meeting his eyes with my moistened gaze, but he looked away. He didn't want to know of my increasing terror. I desperately had to think of something to escape this all too familiar situation. I had to act fast, because any second he was about to rape me. *Please, please help me up there. Give me something I can use to escape this.*

I had become better at reading my little inklings in my gut that whispered to me when I needed them the most, and at that very moment after pleading to the sky, I received the most unusual, yet simplest of messages. *Delay him first, that's your escape.* The idea switched on like a light bulb, and I dropped instantly back into my body. It was now crystal clear; I needed to stall him until I could think of something else, buying myself more time.

I didn't have another second to deliberate on whether it would work, so I blurted out, "Okay, okay, I'll have sex with you, but could you just wait? Wait, please, just for a second."

Miraculously he paused, blinking his eyes in a suspended state of anticipation, waiting for further instructions.

This was my one and only golden opportunity, so I continued. "Wouldn't it be better if we did this later? Because right now my friend will be getting worried about why I'm taking so long, and she'll either come looking for us or report me missing."

His head cocked to one side like a golden retriever so I kept going. "It's just that she gets panicky if I am ever missing for more than ten minutes, and she is the type that will get security." *He isn't going to buy a word of this, surely.*

To my astonishment, he *was* listening, actually, dumb-as-a-stump, listening.

I almost had him, but I needed to seal the deal. "I wouldn't want you to get in any kind of trouble, so we had better wait until later."

He held his pause. I couldn't believe that he looked as though he was actually buying my line. His eyes softened, and his face relaxed. He *was*!

Now I had to really sell it, so I closed with, "How about I meet you later? That way we can have more time, and it will be better when nobody is likely to burst in on us?" Clutching my breath, anticipating that he would realize any second what I was doing, I silently and desperately prayed that my words would work. They did!

He lifted himself off me and flung his legs over the side of the bunk, sitting upright on the edge. I couldn't read his thoughts, but I didn't care because he had stopped, and I was spared.

"Later then," he said, rising to his feet. He walked towards the door and left through it without turning back.

My heart still pounding as I sat up, I slipped into our tiny shower and sat on the floor of it, turning on the water and letting the warmth cascade over me. I had to wash away his grubby residue. Although I felt somewhat relieved, I also felt sick. I started sobbing. I cried for every messed-up thing that these types of guys had ever put me through. I thought of my ex-flatmates, the fucker who raped me, and those who continued to grab at me and yell out at me. My anguished tears fell until I felt numb enough to slip into a soft, hypnotic trance, quietly pacified by the gentle caress of the water.

I dried, dressed myself and waited a bit longer before I returned. I wanted to make certain that he was absolutely long gone. Narrowly escaping another rape was a miracle, and I knew it would be foolish of me to place all my faith and hope in that delay tactic working every time.

Despite being spared the horrendous nightmare of another forceful penetration, I still had to live with the assault that *did* take place. The defilement of my breasts, my skin, my mouth, and the violation of the most personal part of me would always remain with me. The terror I felt from what took place in my cabin would linger forever.

When I finally had the courage to return to the deck, those Sydney boys had left, and Natalie was playing a spirited game of table tennis with another young man. I waited for her on a deck chair. When she finished, she came over and asked me what took me so long. I felt the words rise into my throat, collecting and piling into a dam, but I stopped them, pressing them against my teeth, blocking them from bursting forth. I couldn't tell her. I feared her response, or rather, her *lack* of response.

I had been assaulted before, and when I shared my ordeal with a friend at that time, it was trivialized and shrugged off as if it were nothing. So a quixotic, boy-crazy girl like Natalie would more than likely react the same way. I couldn't take that. I swallowed my words and instead gave off my fake "I'm fine" smile.

The remainder of the voyage I spent whipping my head around with edgy jolts of mind trickery, thinking I spotted my attacker everywhere. Luckily, I never ran into him again. I did, however, have to plan dozens of tactical manoeuvres to avoid being cornered again by those who had me in their sights. Strangely, it was easier to hear, "How's it goin'? Wanna root?" At least they were upfront about what they wanted. It was the silent ones, the devious schemers who planned to trap me, strip me of my free will and take what wasn't theirs who I was most afraid of.

The trip was a colossal disappointment, nothing like I had imagined, and although the islands were gorgeous when I first saw them, I had lost all interest in exploring them. I wanted to be home in my bed, under the protective feathers of my goose down. This was far from the thrilling and dazzling adventure I was expecting from my first time abroad. If I ever got the chance to travel again, it definitely wasn't going to be on a cruise.

Chapter 11

With no home of my own and an inadequate income, I did what I had to in order to survive. I often had to grab work quickly; my growling tummy didn't allow me the option of holding out for something better. If I needed somewhere to live, I couldn't be too picky about the location or who I shared with. All I knew was, male flatmates were at the very bottom of my list.

After returning from the cruise, I needed to find work as soon as possible. I accepted a job as a phone operator in an office with about twenty other staff, who also dreamed of brighter futures. Most were friendly, many were my age, and a few invited me to socialize with them occasionally. Having become jaded by the debauchery of "the glitter strip" in Surfers Paradise, a bunch of us planned a night out in Brisbane, again thinking "the big smoke" would have more to offer. The girls and I were hoping for a better selection of men and perhaps more culture and civility as well. Five of us decided to drive up on a Saturday night.

Dressed in our best dancing gear, we chatted, giggled and sang out of tune while we followed the long band of tar along the M1 motorway until the glowing metropolis crested over the hill. We had our choice of places to go, and we settled on one small club that we liked the look of. The band was playing some of our favourite tunes, and the crowd was sparse enough for us be fairly safe from groping hands.

Sixty minutes later, I was clutching a bathroom sink, staring at the blood caked on my face in the mirror of the ladies room. Tears formed tiny rivulets that streamed down my cheeks, gathering up blood and dripping into the white enamel bowl. With a dull thud in my head that mimicked a heartbeat, I scanned my skin and hair for any remaining fragments of shattered glass. I was trembling from having just been terrorized, all because I showed courtesy to the wrong guy.

My workmates and I had been watching the band when the sandy-haired young man said hello. He was not unattractive, but from his course vocabulary and troublemaker eyes, I could tell he was someone I needed to keep at arm's length. We exchanged pleasantries, and I remained polite but didn't give too much away, hoping he'd move on. He didn't. He continued to hang around making small talk.

My friends eyed me and mouthed, "Who's that?" to which I shrugged, "I don't know." They didn't like the uninvited guest either, so they gestured that they were going to move to another part of club. I nodded and went to go with them.

"Hey, where ya goin'?" the bothersome boy asked curtly, as if entitled to know. Now I really didn't like him.

"Oh, I'm just going with my friends over there. I'll see you later." I shouldn't have even said that much. He somehow now had the impression that I owed him more. Unable to bare the rejection of being ditched I suppose, he blocked me from leaving.

"Before you go, how's 'bout a dance?"

The last thing I wanted to do was give this guy any reason to think I was interested in him, but then I had another thought. *If I do this one thing, then he should leave me alone, right?*

My older generation parents taught me from a young age, if you show courtesy towards others, most people should treat you in kind. That may be the case with some, and more relevant in their day, but I hadn't yet learned that wasn't how the world worked these days. It certainly wasn't the case with this guy. I was not aware that my good manners were going to be seen as a weakness to be taken advantage of.

After making the mistake of dancing with him to one song, not only wasn't he willing to let me go, but he fell under the false notion that I owed him even more. As I went to leave, he stopped me again.

"Ya reckon you can give us a lift home later?"

Is he serious? No I don't want to drive some guy I just met home. I have to drive my own friends home. Man, I hate this position.

"Oh, I can't promise anything," I answered stupidly. I just wanted to leave. I walked away and joined my friends. I tried to enjoy myself but just felt like someone's prey.

After about twenty minutes, we all decided to leave. We slipped out the back door and made our way down to the underground parking lot. As we climbed into the car, which belonged to our friend, we heard a loud, rough voice shout out at us.

"Where d'ya think you're goin'?" It was him. He had followed us and brought three of his tough-looking buddies along with him. He was fast approaching and now at the side of the car. "Hey, you were supposed to take me home!" he snapped with hostility.

We all stiffened with worry.

"Just start the engine and go!" my friends urged. I was in the driver's seat, the designated driver as usual. Assuring myself I had enough time, I slid the key into the ignition, but before turning it, I reached for the seat belt without thinking.

Just at that moment, an arm appeared inside the vehicle. He had slipped it in through the open window, and he was now reaching for the keys. I reacted without thinking and reached out and grabbed onto the keys just before he got to them. He grabbed my hand, and we became involved in a struggle. I was so frightened of what he was going to do.

The more we fought, the more I panicked, and I gripped my hand tighter around them. He squeezed my hand harder and kept applying more and more pressure. I couldn't take the crushing pain a moment longer and finally had to let the keys drop to the floor. I was mortified. I reached down to retrieve them immediately, but my hands were so shaken that I couldn't quite grasp them. I fumbled around and around but was unable to get hold of them securely. He was grabbing my arm, squeezing it and trying his best to screw up my chances of claiming ownership.

"Forget the keys, Joy, just roll up your window!" my friends shouted with urgency. I sprang back up and grabbed onto the handle of the window winder. I frantically cranked it up as hastily as I could. His arm was still inside the car but I kept winding it up onto his forearm anyway, thinking, *Oh shit he isn't going to like this!* He had no choice but to retract his arm, and the second he did, I madly finished cranking the window all the way up. I momentarily felt slightly relieved that I was finally safe.

"Fucking bitch!" he screamed out, his fist smashing through the window, causing the glass to shatter, while his knuckles followed through into the side of my face.

Thousands of glass fragments exploded with a mighty bang and flew in every direction, as if a bomb had just detonated. I sat, paralyzed in shock and absolute horror. I lifted my hand to my face to feel for what damage he had caused with the impact of his blow. My cheek felt numb, tender and wet. It was my blood.

"Joy, you're bleeding!" my friends bellowed.

Without hesitation, our most spirited and gutsy associate and owner of the car leapt out of her side door and gave chase to my assailant, who bolted off up the ramp with his miscreant mates, scattering in every direction. The rest of us sat in shock, unable to move or speak. She trudged back thirty seconds later, shrugging her shoulders, defeated.

"They've gone," she panted.

One by one, my equally terrified friends climbed out of the car, but I was stuck, imprisoned by countless glimmering slivers of razor-sharp chips. There was no way we could drive away in that state. Slowly and delicately, I was assisted out from the debris. We returned upstairs to the club to report the incident to security and to tend to my wounds.

I washed the blood from my face and assessed the damage. The cuts and scratches weren't as bad as they looked, nothing too deep, I was more shaken than anything and furious with myself for not seeing it coming. I should have known better.

As I stared back at myself in the mirror, I shook my head in utter disillusionment with the Australian male species. As I dabbed my cuts with a moistened Kleenex, I spoke to my reflection, "Don't you ever give them any opportunity to do this to you again."

We reported the incident to the security officer, who assured us he would look into it. We never heard another word from him, or anyone, about the matter again. There was no follow-up whatsoever, and that young punk was never caught, never charged and got away scot-free. What good is security if they don't keep you secure? My friend's car window was toast; our big night out was trashed, and my nerves were just about shot.

By simply being born female, it felt that I had a lifetime of limitations placed upon my rights as a human being. One of the rights I was often denied, it seemed, was the right to feel safe. There was never a day that I didn't receive some form of harassment, feel threatened, or feel at risk of some male inflicting harm upon me. If I had been born male, I doubt I would have had to experience such things, especially not on a daily basis. I wondered if they really knew how draining and tedious it was to never feel safe and to always have a knot in your stomach from having to be continually on guard. Would they treat women any differently if they understood what they put us through?

It was like I was fighting my own personal war with an enemy that often disguised itself as a fellow human being. How was it fair that by being even remotely attractive, I had no right to feel secure, to be taken seriously as a person, or to be treated with respect and be left alone? I felt completely drained.

* * *

When life parceled out cruelties, it was vital that I reconnect with nature. One of the most gentle and cleansing places I could turn to was the beach. I loved the simple joy it brought me to be idle in the sun and absorb the soothing warmth into my skin. Swirling my toes around in the delicate, pale sand and meditating on the gentle splashes of the waves provided magical time for self-reflection and quiet healing. As long as I had my hat and my sunblock, I could happily stay put for hours.

Shortly after that incident, face tender and still feeling rather rattled, I went and lay face down on my beach towel, trying to recover from the trauma. A shadow came over me. Looking up, I saw a tall, ginger-haired male hovering over me, completely naked with a full erection. He had dropped his towel and was standing there, two inches from my body, shielding the sun with his hands and looking out to sea. He must have been around fifty years old.

What the hell? My eyes widened with horror. *What the heck is this guy planning to do? How do I get rid of this creep?* Fear surged through my veins.

It is impossible to know what goes through men's brains when they do twisted things like these. Never knowing what is in store for you as an unsuspecting target makes the fear you experience that much more intense. You don't know whether you are going to be the victim of indecent exposure, at the lower end of the scale, or the victim of rape, beating or murder at the other. You just don't know what their plans are. Because these individuals are screwed up in the head, you worry that they could be capable of anything. That is the most frightening part—the *anything*.

My heart pounded brutally in my chest, as I feared the worse. I laid my head back down and prayed for a miraculous rescue. With my breath coming in gasps, I tried to remain as still and frigid as possible, willing him away. I gripped the top corner of my beach towel and squeezed it tightly in my palm, praying and willing, not moving a muscle, expecting to feel his unwanted touch at any moment. Nothing was happening.

I continued to lie completely motionless for what seemed like an eternity, but in reality it would have been around sixty seconds. When you are engulfed in panic, one second can feel like forever. Still nothing. *Strange.*

I relaxed my grip on the towel and drew in a gravelly breath, preparing myself. I lifted my head and looked up. Nobody was there. He had disappeared.

After a slow and controlled exhale, the panic started to subside. I sat up. I looked about everywhere, but he was nowhere to be seen.

Perhaps I foiled his plans. Maybe he was out to terrorize and shock girls like me all up and down the beach, and because he didn't get the reaction he wanted out of me, he couldn't get his sick, perverted kicks. Maybe he moved on to look for other victims.

It didn't even enter my mind to report that man, I wasn't exactly sure it was even a crime. Nobody had taught me what was, and what wasn't a crime in situations like that. I had so much to learn. If I had known that indecent exposure was actually a crime, I could have used that to potentially scare them off. Of course I know that *now*.

Any attractive female who wanted to enjoy the beach ran the risk of having some sleazy pervert approach her, and the horny, the creepy and the dangerous would troll up and down the coast hunting for females just like us. Men, both young and old, were on the prowl for girls. Many of my friends had similar things happen. They relayed their stories of men approaching them on the sand and asking for head jobs, or for quickies in the dunes or to be watched masturbating.

A few weeks after that incident, I was again lying on my towel, trying to unwind from the street harassment I had received earlier that day. I was also waiting for my brother's girlfriend to collect me when she was ready to go shopping. A young guy came along. He was in his early twenties, I guessed, lean and average looking without much expression.

"Hey there, d'ya mind if I say hello?"

I did mind. I wanted to be left alone, but because he was polite, and I was unsure how to deal with the situation, I felt obliged to say yes. It was exactly the opposite of what I promised myself not to do. He plopped himself down beside me on the sand.

"So, are ya from around 'ere?" he asked.

I don't know why, but I decided to give him the benefit of the doubt that he may have just been looking for someone to talk to while enjoying the beach.

"Yes, I live not too far from here. Yourself?" I politely replied.

"Oh me? Yeah, I'm on holidays from Shepparton. Just stayin' in these apartments up 'ere," he pointed behind us to a fifteen-floor high-rise only twenty metres away.

"Oh, I have family that live only a few miles from Shepparton!" I smiled.

"Oh, sweet!

We paused for what seemed like fifteen seconds or so.

So, ya wanna come up for . . . some coffee?" he asked.

Coffee? On such a hot day? That's a bit odd.

"Oh, it's a bit too hot for coffee, but thanks anyway." I didn't hesitate to answer.

"Ya sure? I've only got about an hour. My wife's out shoppin', and I got the place to meself."

Oh really? Oh, okay, so coffee means sex, *gotcha! Does he honestly think I will jump at the chance to rush off with a complete stranger, a married guy, alone, and with the risk of his wife returning and turning mental? What is he, nuts?* I felt anxious, worried and harassed all at once, and it all knotted in my gut.

"Oh, I'm good here thanks." I just wanted him to go away now.

"Okay, you don't have to have coffee. What about a beer or

. . . well . . . me?" he smirked.

Just fuck off will you, and leave girls alone, you sick fuck. You have a wife, you low-life cheater. I bet she would love to know what her husband gets up to when she's not around, and I would really love to be the one to tell her. The audacity of this guy!

"No, I'm okay thanks, I have a friend meeting me any minute, and when she gets here, we are going to go shopping," I explained.

At that moment, I spotted her walking down the pathway, like a guardian angel sent to save me, just in the nick of time.

"Here's my friend now, so I'm going, bye," I said quickly.

As we left the beach, my brother's girlfriend teased me about having a new potential boyfriend. I rolled my eyes and couldn't get away fast enough. That guy had no interest in being anyone's "boyfriend."

Joy Jennings

Chapter 12

When my sister, Julie, was on one of her return trips to the coast, she made lunch plans with her old school friend, Trudie. She was visiting from Melbourne to have a brief holiday, accompanied by her parents and the man in her life. Mum was invited too, and at the last minute, I ended up tagging along. We met at the arranged place, ordered our food and sat down to eat.

Trudie was a large-breasted, chatty girl with a partner much older than herself—at least twenty-five years her senior, maybe more.

After a while, I noticed Mum's behaviour suddenly and dramatically change. Her usual soft and friendly expression almost vanished as she jerked back in her wheelchair. *Has she seen a ghost?* It was extraordinarily odd. I'd never seen anything rattle my mother that way.

A minute later, the penny dropped, and my heart sank at the realization of what she had reacted so badly to. Oh my goodness, this was *that* girl. *That* friend of my sister's who took refuge with our family all those years ago. And this was *that* father of hers, that low-life pedophile she was hiding from back then. *Oh no, Mum has just twigged, and so have I. Holy crap!*

When Julie was around sixteen, and I was eleven, Trudie stayed with us for about a week. As my sister and I were sharing a room then, I couldn't help overhearing their late-night, teary conversations. My sister was always so caring of others, continually taking people under her wing and befriending everyone who needed a shoulder. She is still the same way today. While her friends would cry rivers, Julie would be the one who would mop up their tears and offer support.

This girl poured out her heart and soul to Julie about how she was being sexually abused by her father. He had been sneaking into her room for years, since she was about thirteen. The reason she was staying in our room *that* week was that she had just found out she was pregnant, to him! She was a complete and utter wreck of a girl, with nowhere to turn. My sister, it seemed, was the only one there for her during, what I'm sure must have been, an unimaginably difficult time.

During her living hell, she was also set upon by a much older married man, who lured her with the promise of a pair of *safe* arms to run into. He began having an affair with her. I'm not sure if she was even of age by then. She fell for this slimy weasel, as he had provided an escape from her father, but the whole time he was sleeping with Trudie, he never left his wife. Trudie, as a result, missed out on her entire youth because she waited and waited for him, while he took advantage of her misguided trust and affections, keeping her hanging in by a thread. From what I could gather by sitting there having lunch with these people, he must have eventually left his marriage, because here they were together, sitting with her parents next to us at the table.

This guy didn't seem to have a problem sitting beside her monster of a father, the very one he helped her get away from. In another shocking realization, neither did her mother. She either didn't know or didn't want to know what her husband had done. It isn't uncommon for mothers to turn a blind eye to the fact that their husbands are molesters. Some just cannot handle the truth, I suppose.

There was nothing remarkable about her dad's appearance. If anything he looked like a sweet, old, fatherly type with a big smile and fond affection for everyone around him. I couldn't reconcile where Trudie's head was at. She was happily chatting away as if nothing were out of the ordinary. Perhaps she had blocked out her past or was too frightened and messed up to know what the hell to do about it.

The situation seemed so incredibly screwed up that I felt too ill to eat, and noticing that Mum couldn't finish her vegetable soup, she must have felt the same. I didn't know what my sister was thinking, but knowing her, she would have been simply maintaining her role as loyal friend, offering support no matter what.

When we finished lunch, they wanted to wander about the high-end designer stores in the mall to window shop. I pushed Mum along in her wheelchair, trailing way behind, unsure about what to do or say. The way in which that man's crimes were being ignored astounded me. If that poor girl was too frightened and damaged to find her voice—which I could relate to a thousand percent—then her mother should have done something. She should have had that man arrested. But if she *honestly* didn't know, then it should have been up to that man friend of hers to step in. By his limited facial expressions and vocabulary, he simply appeared indifferent to her plight.

This so-called father should have been showing nothing but remorse while rotting in jail for the rest of his life. Instead here he was, displaying nothing but exuberance while eyeing Gucci watches and Versace sunglasses without a care in the world—a world that was increasingly off its axis.

* * *

My sister, Kerry, and her husband broke up later that same year. She said he was verbally abusive, and I believed her, but I don't recall discussing it with her in detail. After a while, she started dating another guy, a tall, strapping young man, who seemed to be a lot of fun. Kerry really liked that in a guy.

On her birthday in late November, the two of us went to a Michael Jackson concert in the city. It totally rocked! I loved that guy. He was so talented and cute back in those days. He was doing his "Bad" tour across the world, and I had one of the best nights of my life. Afterwards, we drove to her new boyfriend's house close by, where apparently we were to be spending the night.

We arrived to what appeared to be the end of a drunken, raucous night, and this new boyfriend and his male flatmates were winding down from an evening of drinking and partying. After a period of awkwardness, a feeling I would get whenever I was in the company of inebriated blokes, it was time to settle down for the night. I was shown a foam camping mattress that was made up on the floor in the front sunroom. I changed into my pyjamas and slipped under the covers.

Muffled giggles echoed from the room next door, and the clinking and clanging of bottles reverberated from the kitchen. The chatter soon died down, and the house became dark, apart from the soft, white glow from the almost full moon gleaming through the window. I heard the timber floorboards begin to creak and a cadence of footsteps drawing closer. I listened intently, trying to figure out where they were headed and then realized they were coming towards me.

Someone slipped into my bed beside me. I could feel a body behind mine, spooning into my back. I assumed it was one of the flatmates. He hugged me tightly, pulling me into a snug embrace, and started nuzzling his face into the back of my neck. My body became as rigid as a gumtree. His foul breath hit my nose with a rotten stench of lager and cigarettes. His fingertips started to flutter along the outline of my pyjama top, tracing my skin, a touch I did not remember inviting. I became gripped in a snare of unwelcomed advances and flushed in a hot sweat.

Although one side of my mind knew I had the safety of my sister and her new beau just in the next room, the other part of my brain, the victimized side, started going into overdrive. *Oh God, what is he going to do to me?*

"Leave her alone, Mick. Go back to your own bed," my saviour's voice called out from the next bedroom. I felt momentarily pacified by the protective voice, but my new bed buddy neither responded nor stopped. He brought his head around in the attempt to kiss me, but I darted my head about to avoid his lips, my "go-to" move I had developed.

"Mick, leave that poor girl alone. I mean it!"

He ignored the demands again. His hands were now sliding towards my breast. While torturing me with his advances, he pressed his groin up against me, making thrusting motions. It terrorized me.

"For the last time, Mick, get the hell out of there. I mean it!"

He finally stopped after that, lifting himself out from the bed and disappearing into the night. I was so incredibly relieved that he left, but in hindsight, I really should have been the one to stand up for myself. I should have kicked that guy so hard in his misters, that it would have made his eyes water for the next three years! I just needed to find the courage from somewhere, somehow.

Not long after that night, I ran into my sister's ex-husband, Glen, at a bar when I was out with my co-workers. For some reason, perhaps assuming I would be flattered, he thought it was appropriate to tell me, "Oh boy, did I used to fantasize about you when I was with your sister!"

Wow, seriously? Having dirty thoughts about me while with my sister, that's just wrong on so many levels. What a sleaze.

"Perhaps you should have kept that one to yourself, Glen. Thanks all the same," I replied as I turned my back and walked away. When I finally looked back, he seemed flabbergasted that I wasn't the least bit interested. What did he expect? Was I supposed to feel privileged that I made it onto his list of sexual fantasies? Not in the least bit.

* * *

My home life was about as unsettled as a spider's web in a broom factory. I was continually on the move. So it was no surprise when I was told I had to move again. The place where I was living had been sold, and the new owners wanted to occupy it—a typical scenario where I lived. The interminable search for a new residence was never easy, and after weeks of house hunting and scrutinizing potential roomies, I decided to take a room in a clean and affordable place close to work.

The problem was I was going to have to share with a bloke as well as another girl. I had resisted living with males since my first experiences at eighteen, but I had run out of time and options.

My new male roommate, Andy, was a house painter who loved his beer and footy, and the girl, Fiona, worked in a bank and lived a party lifestyle, so she was rarely home. When Andy was home, he sat around drinking and getting high, smoking cigarettes and watching sports. He went to bed nightly around ten o'clock and was gone before I woke in the morning.

Being only a two-level apartment building, I would often see the same neighbours coming and going. One neighbour, a thirty-something-year-old roofer who lived upstairs, was commissioned to fix our roof that was in need of repairs. I encountered him one morning when he was working on the roof, and we exchanged simple pleasantries. The following morning, we said hello again as I was leaving for work and greeted each other every morning that week. He appeared to be a friendly, genuine, not-bad-looking guy with a nuance of charisma, a combination that seemed Aussie tradies rarely exuded.

At the end of the week, I went to say good morning on my way past, but realizing my shoe needed adjusting, I bent down to fix it. As I did, he called down to me, "Oi where's my hello?"

I looked up, ready to give him a greeting, but was shocked to find him pulling his shorts aside to flash his nuts at me. He was grinning that same smirk I had seen many times. I hated that smirk. It confused and terrorized me. Did he think it was some kind of innocuous gesture to show his Aussie charm? If I had known more about the law at the time, I could have taught him a thing or two about appropriate greetings, but I was so shocked and horrified, I simply ran to my car and tried to avoid him from then on.

Another person I had to start trying to elude was my flatmate, Andy. He had become way too involved in my life, especially regarding my appearance. It started with small comments, mostly about what I wore, how my shoes looked, or the way in which I styled my hair, as if he had a vested interest, or as if it were his business. He then started asking me where I was going, who I was seeing, what I was planning to wear to Christmas dinner with my family and things along those lines. It was unnerving. I never once asked for his opinions, yet he kept giving them regardless.

One evening, I was sitting on my bed reading, and I could sense there was something wrong. My gut always warned me of danger, and I felt I was being watched. I looked up to see him peering at me through the crack where the door was ever so slightly ajar. It frightened me initially, the ordeal with that eye peering through my neighbour's fence came flooding back, but then upon seeing that it was him, I felt a small comfort that it was at least somebody I knew. I was momentarily deluded, thinking I was actually safe. I then became angry with myself for not thinking to shut my door tight, but I had assumed he was out in the living room, stoned and zoned out like usual. I didn't expect him to be silently creeping up the hallway.

"Hey yooou!" he said as he opened the door wider. "I see you're wearing that sexy singlet you *know* turns me on!" he said suggestively.

I do? It does? That's news to me! Okay, now I started to feel sick and worried.

"Can I help you with something, Andy?" I asked, grabbing for my blanket.

"Oh, come on now. You know what you do to me," he

answered, moving further into my room. I jumped from the bed, sidestepping him and slipped into my bathroom. It was the quickest escape I could find.

He followed me in.

Oh God, no.

"Um, Andy perhaps you'd better go back to your TV. I think you might be mistaken," I told him, scared witless.

"You do realize what you do to me, don't you?" he continued, gesturing for me to look down at the bulge in his dirty pants.

My mouth went dry, my scalp prickled and I felt like I had thousands of fire ants crawling under my skin. He had now backed me up as far as I could go, and I was leaning up against my vanity. He came in closer, putting his arms on each side of the sink, trapping me in. His red, vacant eyes, the same ones I'd see in those who were stoned or drunk or both, looked me up and down, focusing on my chest and smelling me like I was his next meal.

"Oh you're such a tease. See what you do to me?" He grabbed my hand and placed it onto his crotch, rubbing it around and stimulating his hard dick with it.

I fought against him, revolted, furious and desperate. If I had thought of it or had the guts, I would have kicked him right where he'd put my hand and told the sleazeball where to go, but all I could think of was getting him to stop, somehow.

"Oh, come on. Keep going. I'm just about to cum!" he urged, forcing my hand to rub him.

With every ounce of strength I had, I reefed my hand away. I grabbed at anything on the sink behind me that I could use to distract him. I felt my fingers brush against my hair comb, so I picked it up and brought it around in front of his face. Wielding it like a weapon, I cried angrily, "Just let me go, Andy!" A lot of good it would have done, it was only plastic for crying out loud.

His eyes widened, appearing suddenly surprised, like my

reaction was the opposite of what he was expecting. He let me go.

I can't believe he thought I wanted this!

He didn't move for me when I pushed him to get away, but he didn't stop me when I slipped out from his clutches.

I bounded out of the bathroom and back into my bedroom towards my closet. I grabbed my dressing gown from within it and wrapped it around me, tightly swaddling myself like a newborn. He left without a fuss, looking confused and disappointed.

Did he seriously think I wanted him? Why do all the males I come across assume they can just take what isn't theirs?

Sitting on my bed, trying to regain composure, I thought back over the past few months I had been living there, searching for signals I must have missed, but there was nothing I could remember doing that he could have possibly misread. Perhaps being polite was enough for him to get the wrong impression, just as it always seemed to be the case.

My head swam in circles for hours, with the distant menacing echoes of all my male flatmates playing over and over in my mind. *Does every one of them have to be a sexual predator?*

I knew I couldn't stay there a moment longer. I packed my things and started to look for another place to live, somewhere I could go to be safe.

My life seemed adrift without an anchor. A normal life—without emotional and physical danger or fear—was beginning to look like an illusion. I wanted desperately to enrich my life with wonderful things and people, and to be filled with hopes and dreams, but instead I was in a constant state of violation, and my dreams were continually being crushed by fear and doubt.

Chapter 13

Part-time in the evenings, I worked an extra job delivering pizzas. I needed to start saving if I was ever to afford my travel dreams. Delivering food to strangers at night had its risks, but I needed the money and thought if I was careful, I would be okay.

A few months into the job, one of our drivers was killed while out on a delivery. It shook us all to the core. He knocked on the front door at the address he was given, and when nobody answered, he walked around the back in the hope they would hear him at the rear. They did, but they mistook him for someone else, someone they wanted dead. The door opened only a crack, just enough for the end of a shotgun to slide through, and it was fired, blowing a gaping hole in the middle of my co-worker's chest. He was killed instantly. He tragically left behind a pregnant wife and a young daughter.

We all became fearful about continuing to work there but stayed, because head office gave us the reassurance we needed when they introduced their new security policies: no back doors; keep our car headlights on; the customer's porch lights must be on; and if anything looks or feels suspicious, keep our engines running.

There were a couple of hairy moments. One male customer asked me to take the pizza inside, and when I did, he closed and locked the door behind me. Naturally I instantly panicked, but he didn't do anything but pay me, perhaps he was just paranoid.

Another man, a bushy, lumbering bloke, offered me dope if I came back after my shift and partook of it with him.

"Thanks, but I can't stand the stuff," I declined.

Another older and smellier guy in his sixties, whose only Friday night kicks was a "Supreme with extra cheese," asked me if I offered *other* services besides food deliveries.

"Nope, just the pizza. Sorry," I answered.

Over the months, I received quite a few proposals of returning after my shift to keep lonely and horny male customers company, all of which I declined. I was surprised just how many late-night businesses wanted pizza too, including brothels and such. If I had been that way inclined, I could have made quite a bit of hush money from what I witnessed on occasion, but I didn't want to get mixed up in any of that.

One evening, I knocked on a door holding a "Meat Lovers, hold the anchovies," and my old flatmates, Samantha and Pete, answered. I hadn't seen them in years. They had obviously moved and now had a young son. I passed them their pizza and caught up on their latest news, but I had to get back. I was surprised they were still together, being that Pete had displayed such audacious behaviour towards me back when I lived with them. Goodness knows how many other girls he had set his sights on since then, or had he changed? Did he finally become a man and decide to be a devoted and faithful partner?

The following evening, while waiting for my "Vegetarian" to come out of the oven, Pete showed up. He pulled up outside the shop in a car that looked like it belonged in a *Mad Max* movie. He waved me over.

"What are you doing here?" I asked, surprised and puzzled.

"Well it's just that when I saw ya last night, it stirred up the old feelings that I had for ya!" he proclaimed, smiling in anticipation.

Oh no! I was stunned into an immediate fearful silence.

"Yeah, so, I left Samantha, and now I'm a free man, so we can pick up where we left off," he announced with surprising confidence.

What the hell? I was flabbergasted! *Is he deluded?*

I was called to deliver my piping hot pizza, so I brushed him off, explaining that I didn't have time to talk. I left him there, sitting in his beast of a car while I set out on my delivery.

"Just think about it!" he called out as I was leaving.

There was nothing to think about. I wasn't interested in him before, so why would I be now? Even more so, the fact that he was capable of leaving his wife and child in a heartbeat over someone who had never shown interest in him before, despite his advances, was shocking. I hated being in this position.

When I returned from my delivery, he was still there, still parked outside my workplace, waiting in his car. I sighed heavily. My job was too demanding for me to give him any attention, so I had to ignore him while I worked. I also had the craziest notion that if I didn't appear interested, he might just get the hint and leave. It had been years, so maybe he had grown up a little and learned how to recognize when someone didn't want him. No such luck. The longer he waited outside, the more it appeared that he didn't get it. He was still hopeful.

When I finished my shift, I knew I had no choice but to face him. I gingerly took the dreaded steps towards his car.

"So have you made your decision?" he raised his eyebrows in anticipation, applying the pressure.

Is this really his way of trying to get a girl to like him, by pressuring her? I took a deep breath. "I don't think so, Pete. I'm busy with two jobs and don't have time for a boyfriend right now," I babbled nervously, eyes darting. I became cranky with myself for lying. I still lugged around such anxiety over men having a bad reaction to rejection. Why do they make it so difficult for us to express simple honesty? If I said I just didn't like him, his ego might fracture, and I could be in trouble. Being taught how to deal with this kind of thing would have been a tremendously helpful skill in life, but who thinks of these things? I really, *really* hated this position.

His eyes glossed over, unfazed and expressionless. My gut twisted tighter. He wasn't getting it. "Goodnight, Pete," I added, walking away.

"I'll give you more time!" he called out.

Oh great, just what I need, a guy who won't take no for an answer. I wondered if he was going to be turning up at my house, or my day job, and what other wild ideas he might have, because after all, he always did like to pursue me.

The following night, when I turned up for my shift, he was already parked outside. I instantly felt irritated, annoyed and harassed, just as I had when he kept coming into my bedroom. However this time, my annoyance actually fuelled the courage I needed to approach him.

"What are you doing here, Pete?" I couldn't believe I had to ask.

"Waiting," he replied smugly.

Waiting for what? A different answer this time perhaps? Why, because he can sit outside my workplace for a super long time? Oh yeah, why didn't I see what a catch he actually was, how impressive!

"I'm working, Pete. I haven't got time to talk to you. I'm sorry," I told him.

"It's okay. I've got all the time in the world!" he smiled haughtily.

I was dumbfounded. It seemed as though the only message he was going to understand was a clear and direct one. I had to work on formulating one. This was not my area of expertise.

My boss called me over, and so I snapped to attention. He told me, in no uncertain terms, that if I didn't get rid of this guy, my job would be in jeopardy. Not only was he taking up valuable customer parking, but he was also distracting me from my work and creeping out the other staff. His hanging around was just simply not on. It was most humiliating and highly embarrassing. Having to explain to my employer that I'd already rejected this guy, but he wasn't leaving, made me feel like an idiot who had no control over my personal life. I shrugged at him, explaining I was at a loss as to how to make this guy get the message.

In fifteen seconds, it was all over. My boss headed directly to the front entrance and called out, "Hey mate, you need to move on. The lady said she wasn't interested, so you need to quit harassing my staff."

Pete instantly sat up straight and started his engine. I held my breath in anticipation. He was leaving! But not without a show first. Being true to form for any young Aussie male, especially those with hoon cars, in an attempt to regain his supremacy, he smoked up his tires and screeched off, tearing up the road for everyone to see and hear. A classic retaliation for having his ego crushed.

What a child. I was just glad he didn't take it out on me.

Males seemed to be such strange, pitiful creatures, always demanding female attention as if entitled to it. If we failed to yield to their demands, they either took what they wanted anyway or acted like babies and took off sulking. I couldn't understand why they respected the wishes of other guys, but not the woman they were supposed to be sweet on. If they really cared about a girl, why would they resort to stalking, hounding, pestering and harassing her? Instead of trying to win a girl over, perhaps with romantic gestures and gentlemanly behaviour, their persistent and creepy methods would only frighten and annoy. It seemed as if it was more about seeking control and ownership than true companionship. That was the quality in men I couldn't stand.

Once the dust had settled, and my honour had been restored in the workplace, I was given a new assignment. We had hired some new drivers, and it was my job to train one of them. The task was easy enough. All I had to do was take my charge out on a few deliveries while he observed.

My rookie was about twenty-five, prone to typical behaviour for a young Aussie guy, and a bit rough around the edges with an air of cocky arrogance, but I assumed he would take his new job seriously. I took him out on a couple of runs and showed him the ropes. He was learning quickly, so I had him running a few deliveries on his own towards the end of the shift.

On our last run for the night, I was stuffing the takings into my waist pouch when I heard the sound of a zipper. It wasn't the zipper on my money bag, but the fly of his pants. I glanced over at my trainee and saw his fly now fully undone with his hand pulling out his half-erect penis. *What the hell?* He started rubbing it and smiling as if impressed with its increasing size.

"Look what I got for ya!" he boasted.

I felt horrified, disgusted, stupefied!

"Put that away," I commanded, enormously proud of myself for using such an authoritative voice for once in my life. Of course, he ignored me.

"Oh come on, aren't ya impressed? He beamed.

With my hand trembling, I somehow managed to turn the key and start the motor. I wrapped my jittery fingers around the gear stick.

"You like that, don't ya!" he said, waving his pink appendage about, attempting to entice me.

I felt a strong urge to kick him out right there and then, but his actions also caused me to be frightened, befuddling me as to what I should do. My brain filled with a thousand possible outcomes, and not one of them looked good.

He grabbed my hand and brought it over towards his erection. I fought against him the entire way. Our hands hovered over it, suspended, struggling in a hand wrestle.

"Ooh yeah, baby. Give it a good tug for me," he chuffed.

I reefed free and pulled back, shooting him the most intense death look I could conjure. I was not happy with my response, but I was scared. I thrust the stick into gear and accelerated away, sickened and panicked.

It wasn't that far back to the store, five minutes at most, but the entire way he continued with his menacing, sick game. "Oh, so you are frigid, are ya? Come on, don't be such a prude!"

When we returned to the pizza shop, I leapt out of my seat with a mighty spring, desperate to get away from him and his atrocious antics. If ever I had a right to report someone for sexual harassment in the workplace, it was then, but I was clouded with uncertainty about what the policy actually entailed. Who exactly did the laws apply to? I didn't know. What kinds of behaviours were considered harassment and what acts could be reported? I had no idea. I also, for some stupid reason, assumed that those rules didn't even apply to me, maybe because men had been inappropriate to me for so long, I thought that silent suffering was just a fate I had to accept.

I did everything wrong. I should have driven straight to the police station right from the beginning while I still had him in the car. When you are frightened and intimidated in that way, your mind doesn't think logically. You think only about getting out of the situation, and you feel totally alone. I wasn't equipped with the knowledge and fortitude I needed to deal with the situation correctly.

The other mistake I made in the aftermath was quitting that job. I didn't need to do that. I could have and should have reported him. Instead I foolishly did myself out of a paycheque and was furious when I realized all of my costly errors. Why did it appear to be so difficult for males to just leave their junk in their pants and simply act like decent members of society?

Sexual harassment was occurring at my day job as well. My seventy-year-old boss, who was forever drooling over eighteen-year-old bikini calendar girls, continually made lewd comments and shared dirty jokes with his old pervert mates who would come into his store. Their conversations were always vile and sexist, taking it for granted that it was quite appropriate to express what they wanted to do to these young ladies sexually. I heard my boss scrutinize and deliberate on every minuscule detail about the girls in the pictures: the size and shape of their breasts, their rear ends, the shapes of their bodies, the width of their noses and the thickness of their lips. Every feature and every flaw was criticized and commented on. Meanwhile he was a white-haired, bushy-browed, fat, slovenly, wrinkly, old geezer with barely any teeth, not to mention being completely void of any charm or manners.

It wasn't easy to work there with all of that going on, but it was when he crept up behind me and nuzzled his nose into the back of my neck that I was pushed to the brink. Working on a printing task, I had my head down when he sauntered up, took a good long sniff and then kissed my neck, saying, "Oh, you smell so beautiful I couldn't help myself!"

I wanted to yell, "Who do you think you are, you dirty old bastard? Don't you know how disgusting you are? Where do you get off . . ?" A lifetime of angry, bitter words rushed into my mind all at once, but they all became jammed. Instead of saying anything, I flicked him away like an annoying bug and continued my work, blinking back my welling tears. I stored them all just under the rim until I got home, where I let them all spill over the edge.

I never returned to that job after that, once again doing the wrong thing and slipping away quietly, letting someone else get away with unacceptable behaviour, while also losing the ability to support myself.

The next few weeks were spent applying for other jobs. My meagre savings started rapidly dwindling, and I was becoming anxious and desperate. I applied for a waitressing position at an Indian restaurant. During my interview, after admitting I didn't have much experience, the fifty-something-year-old owner tilted his head sideways and began studying me intently. I focused my eyes on the turban on his head, avoiding his uncomfortable ogling. He then bluntly remarked, "Don't look at me with those big blue eyes, it makes me want to kiss you!"

Really? If he is that inappropriate at an interview,

imagine what he's like on a late shift!

He offered me the job, but I declined, preferring to go hungry.

My succession of rusty old cars that were always in need of repair often left me relying on the bus to get around. A week later, riding the bus to another job interview, an elderly gentleman boarded at a stop and began tottering towards the empty seat next to me. As the bus was more empty than full, I figured the dear old-timer was just after some company. He was about to sit down beside me when the bus jolted as it took off, causing the frail old man to lose his balance and fall. The few of us on board assisted him up, for which he was very grateful, although terribly embarrassed.

I felt sorry for the poor old sweetheart, so I chatted to him for the duration of our ride, attempting to make him feel less embarrassed about what had happened. I talked to him about my mother in her wheelchair and the challenges she faced every day.

My stop was approaching, so I rose and said goodbye to the sweet man. He smiled in return, thanking me for being so nice to him. To my astonishment he then added, "I'd love to repay your kindness. How about a roll around in the hay together darlin'?"

Did I hear that right?

"Oh, I'd love to get my hands on a pretty girl like you!"

Yep, he is hitting on me! Oh my! I was so stunned that I couldn't even respond. I shook my head as I stepped off the bus and left for my interview completely blindsided, forgetting everything I had prepared for.

"So where do you see yourself in five years?" a sharply dressed man asked with fingers steepled together upon the desk.

"Having enough money so I don't have to catch the bus!" I blurted without thinking. When I got a call back, I was shocked. I was told I had impressed them with my ambition. I suppose I had that old man to thank for it, dirty old bastard.

Chapter 14

Over the next weeks and months, it was clear that my normal functioning as a human being in the world had been distorted. I could only see a predator in every male. Making the simplest of decisions had become quite complex. No longer being able to relax and enjoy life, I was reduced to basing every decision solely upon my safety. Any time I planned to go anywhere, I had to carefully calculate the risks of being harassed or assaulted.

It was imperative that I considered everything: who I would and wouldn't talk to, which path to walk, which road to drive on, where to park, what time to go out, what time to come home, what I needed to carry with me, what I would wear and how I used my body language. A lot of times, I chose to simply stay home.

It may be commonplace for women to take those precautions anyway, but it is something men never have to worry about, and they don't understand how complicated and exhausting it is. I couldn't even smile at a guy anymore without it being taken out of context. Any slight upturn at the corners of my mouth they would often mistake as romantic interest. My attempt at mere cordiality towards males would be returned with offers of lurid sex acts in toilet cubicles, kinky times in hot tubs, or invitations to follow some stranger back to his house for goodness knows what. Even sharing a few harmless, clean jokes with someone from work would be taken as an interest in them either romantically or sexually. If I exhibited any approachability, they would then take the opportunity to hit on me.

My life had become one of protection, precaution, apprehension and anxiousness. I felt deprived of a carefree life, one where I could experience friendly, pleasant exchanges with the opposite gender, without it being twisted into something sexual.

My parents and I would often watch old Hollywood

movies from the forties and fifties, which I adored. I was spellbound by the simplicity of that era. It was a time of innocence, and I loved watching those young men exhibit real manners and charm. They cherished their ladies with a proper courting process, taking them on real dates with dinner and dancing. Romantic gestures, flowers, letters, poems and songs, I simply adored being swept up in the enchantment of it all. How wonderful it must have been to stroll in the moonlight in the arms of a young man with honourable conduct, without the worry of assault. I ached for that.

I knew better than to expect that type of treatment, knowing there was nothing left that embodied that age gone by, but I certainly did not deserve to be physically confronted with threatening behaviour every time I wanted to go out and enjoy myself.

On a night out with one of my co-workers, my chatty friend became involved in a conversation with a young man. It left his dodgy-looking mate and me obligated to talk to each other. I hated that situation. It always felt forced and awkward. I had been going to great lengths not to start any conversation with a guy that I didn't like the look of, but I still had a very difficult time being rude to people.

I don't recall how the horrible subject started, but this guy, who had forgotten to zip up his fly after using the mens' room, started telling me about how easy it would be to kill another person with his bare hands. It was a morbid and childish topic, better left for pub talk with his buddies, but he must have thought his tough talk was impressing me. I smiled politely, and I guess from sheer boredom, I stupidly challenged his theory. "It couldn't be *that* easy," I said.

The very next second, his two hands lashed out and grabbed my throat, squeezing it hard. He obviously felt the need to demonstrate his point. His grip was very powerful, clutching my neck so tightly that my windpipe was starting to crush. I became so panicked so quickly that the last pockets of air stored in my lungs expelled. I was unable to draw any more breath. Everything in the room rapidly morphed into a dizzy swirl of grey haze. I lifted my hands to his, trying to pry his fingers from around my throat, but I was no match for his strength. He kept them securely in place until his pathetic, ridiculous point was proven, and he wasn't going to let go until he felt vindicated. I was now in real danger, and he knew it.

With his callous eyes boring into mine with vicious cruelty, the sick freak sneered at me through his gritted teeth, and I could feel myself slipping into a dark tunnel. Everything started to fade, and every sound was as if I had cotton balls in my ears. I was mere seconds from losing consciousness.

"Hey man, go easy," his friend nudged, urging him to let go.

My friend, now seeing what was happening, dashed over. "Stop, you idiot!" she cried.

He released his death grip, and I slumped to the floor. I gasped for air, spluttering and gagging, trying to gulp oxygen back into my lungs, sucking in as much life force as I could. Never had I appreciated life so much as at that very moment, and never had I been so scared. I was only seconds away from dropping, and that a**hole didn't care. He didn't care about anything but his own ego.

We had to get the hell away from him as fast as we could and left immediately. Neither of us thought about reporting him. If I had known about the crime of physical assault, I could have, and should have, made him accountable for his actions. I was just desperate to get away and unaware of so much of the world.

* * *

The months after that, the sense of distortion in my life increased. I felt messed up in an essential way, detached from the person I had planned to be. When I caught myself in the mirror, my image felt as though it belonged to somebody else, somebody I had very little in common with. The strength and fortitude I might have once had to fight for myself was slipping away. I wasn't the person I knew anymore. I couldn't find or keep a job or any place to live where I felt safe, and the ideas I had about living life to the fullest were fading. I felt I belonged to them now.

Later that year, I found new hope when I met Alan. Although I had almost given up all hope of finding someone to love and who would love me, I quickly became taken with him. He had a raw energy that drew me in. He wanted to be successful and embraced life, which was delightfully refreshing. He had a passion in him that I found inspiring, giving me the chance to feel invigorated about life once again. I drew upon it, and for the first time in a long time, I felt giddy with the notion that I had found the one.

I fell head over heels. We moved in together within a few weeks. I knew I felt more for him than he did for me, but I thought in time he would be as lost in me as I was in him, once he saw the depths to which I could love him. His friends, however, were nothing like him, which left me questioning why he would associate with them at all.

Two in particular were extremely boisterous, often mouthing off in the company of girls. Somehow, they would always involve me in their ridiculous antics. They would think it absolutely hilarious to expose themselves to me or to call out, "Show us your tits!" as I lay on the beach.

They often touched me inappropriately and loved to make disgusting gestures with their mouths, tongues and fingers, nudging each other with pride afterwards. Being that they were approaching thirty, one would have expected them to have matured by that age, but they continued to egg each other on like nine-year-olds.

On one occasion, I was giving these two particular friends a lift. One was sitting behind me in the back seat, and the other was in the passenger seat next to me. They starting becoming silly, as usual, and talking about some stripper they were both *sharing*. I didn't feel it was necessary to respond. All I could manage was a tight-lipped smile that never met my eyes.

"Yeah, we like strippers. They are hot," they both said. "You'd make a great stripper."

I ignored them, trying to concentrate on driving.

"Ooh yeah, you'd love to get your kit off for all the blokes wouldn't ya?" they continued.

I scowled at them, shaking my head in disapproval of their nonsense.

"Yeah, you do. You want to strip for us dontcha? We can tell," they snickered.

Being Alan's friends, I wasn't sure how much I was supposed to put up with, but I was reaching my limit. As I pulled up to a red traffic light, they chanted, "Come on, getcha gear off then!" They both grabbed onto my top, one arm reaching from behind and one from beside me, both ripping it in one quick motion.

I jolted into a sudden shock as my top tore open. It was the *only* day that I hadn't worn a bra. The *only* day that I had washed every one I owned. Earlier, when I had dashed out to take Alan's satchel to him, I didn't expect to run into to these two clowns and be asked to drive them to their mate's place, so I was caught.

"Ooh baby, nice rack! That's it, shake those boobies about for us then!" they bantered.

I felt a surge of furious volcanic heat filling me. With wild fury, I fumbled around trying to cover myself. Pulling away from the traffic light, I held what I could over me, but I knew I was still somewhat exposed while trying to steer the car without veering off the road or crashing.

I fought back the tears that wanted to flood my face. I wasn't going to let them get to me. I didn't want them to see how sensitive I really was. I needed to tough this out, maybe even try to go along with the joke and try to see the funny side. I swallowed it all, every torturous and violating moment of it, but I failed in every way to see the humour in it.

Thankfully I didn't have to drive them much farther, and soon they instructed me to pull over.

"Just drop of us here. This'll do," they ordered.

I pulled up where they wanted to be dropped off.

"Thanks, gorgeous," one of them said. "I swear, if you weren't with Alan, you'd know about it!"

Know about what? What the hell is that supposed to mean? I didn't cry. I didn't allow myself. I wanted to be strong like I was supposed to be, so I drove back home with a lump in my throat and a top that was now completely ruined.

I tried telling Alan that I didn't like his friends' behaviour, but like my first boyfriend, Mitchell, he didn't seem to think anything they did was such a big deal. I tried to put the matter behind me, but I really needed Alan to care. I brought it up one day when we were standing in the kitchen making a cup of tea. I asked him why he would hang out with those buffoons, when they were so unlike him in every way.

"Why should I have to get rid of my friends?" he snapped.

"I didn't say you have to get rid of them as friends, but they have no right to touch me the way they do, or rip my shirt open, or show me their dicks. Can't you see that it's not funny and actually quite disrespectful?" I tried explaining.

"You can't tell me what to do," his voice escalated.

"Alan, I'm just saying that I don't like it. Isn't that important to you?"

"Oh, they are just having a bit of fun, geez!" he deflected, agitated.

I had just poured myself a hot cup of tea, so I picked it up, took a small sip and continued to hold onto the cup. "Alan, it may be fun for them, but it's not funny to me, and I'd like it if you could care, maybe even defend my honour."

"Don't come between me and my friends," he retorted with a loud bark. Then with one quick motion, he flicked the teacup so that the boiling liquid splashed up all over my chest. It burned me instantly. I scrambled for the sink and splashed cold water over myself.

Alan stood rigid, arms folded, showing no remorse whatsoever. I had no clue how to react. I was overwhelmed with utter shock and horror, hurting both physically and emotionally, but I didn't know what to do. I expected at that point that he would simply walk away, satisfied that he'd inflicted pain upon me and made his point. He was usually so mild tempered, so it was quite alarming that he took it to that level. But he didn't leave. He continued to stand, cemented and stubborn, without concern or regret.

Okay, if this is his game, then I am not prepared to play it.

I wiped the mess from myself, the floor, and the bench, and then calmly poured a new cup of tea, hoping we could just forget what happened. When I finished pouring the boiling water into my cup, he immediately picked it up off the counter and threw that one over me as well.

It burned me even worse that time. I ran out of the kitchen, down the hall and into the bathroom. I jumped in the shower, clothes and all, turning the cold water tap on full blast. When the water started to cascade over my burns, and the sting started to subside, tears flooded my eyes and spilled out in disbelief and sadness. *This is the man I love. What in the hell just happened?*

I heard the door slam. As I stood in the shower, I tried to process. I was shocked, angry, sad and powerless all at once. Grim visions haunted me with the memory of those a**holes ripping my shirt off, and the tears that I didn't shed that day, added to the flow. I also cried from Alan's lack of caring. I cried from the pain of the scalding tea and the horror of what just happened. I cried because it seemed that no man, not even the one who was supposed to love me, was ever going to protect me. I also cried because, at that moment, I realized he couldn't have really loved me.

Eventually, the cool water dissolved my tears. I stepped out and dried myself. I checked my burns in the mirror and saw they would need some treatment. It wasn't until later that the full impact of the sting really set in, and it throbbed and hurt more than when it first happened. Ironically, it was a lot like my life.

I came to a decision to let it go. I decided to take some advice I was given years ago. I was told that forgiveness is a part of loving someone, whether they ask for it or not or deserve it or not, and if the relationship is worth saving, then you need to be prepared to be the bigger person. So I did just that, hoping that it was an isolated incident.

It seemed to be, at least until well into our second year. That's when we had our second argument. We were sitting parked in my car in town. He wanted the car keys. I think he wanted to drive because I had been teaching him. I didn't let go of them, because I felt he wasn't ready to drive on the highway. That must have bruised his ego. He started punching my arm, hard. It hurt, very much. Because he did that, I held onto the keys even tighter. He then closed his fist and really let me have it, punching me hard on my arm. It stung like I couldn't believe. *Why do I always seem to fight with men over car keys?*

It escalated, and I hit him back, only to get him to stop, not because I wanted to hurt him, as if I could anyway. It was a pathetic scene, and two people in another car saw us. They pointed and looked, appearing aghast. I was so humiliated and embarrassed that such a stupid thing got so out of hand. I had to stop it.

"Alan, stop!" I begged, shaken and breathless.

"Fine, get your way. You drive. Go on, drive then. Take me home," he sulked.

I ended up letting that incident go as well. Two flare-ups in two years didn't seem that bad, and I could handle it. Over the following weeks and months, he became somewhat cold and distant. He started behaving differently, spending more time away from me than with me, coming home at all hours, being detached and withdrawn. I was losing him, and I was clueless as to why.

The night he didn't come home at all was when I knew I deserved some answers. When he tiptoed in at six o'clock in the morning, I was both relieved because he wasn't dead or lying in a gutter somewhere and angry that he had stayed out all night. After twenty minutes of vague answers, deflections and avoidance of the truth, I finally braced myself for what I knew I was about to hear. "Alan, are you seeing someone else?"

He nodded silently and shamefully, staring at his feet.

It was as if the earth had split in two, and I tumbled uncontrollably, deep into its obsidian crevices. He finally confessed that he had been having an affair with a friend of mine, someone I had known and thought I could trust. All of our mutual friends and associates had apparently also known about this affair for quite some time, yet I was the last to find out. I felt like an idiot. There was nothing more humiliating to me at that point, than to be the only oblivious person amongst them all, and I was made to look like a fool. I had not only lost the love of my life but also my friends, along with my trust in humanity.

It took what seemed an eternity to get over the agony of the betrayal and the loss of so much. My eyes stung with tears of anger and sadness. Something new inside me perished, leaving me in utter darkness. I would have to pick up and start over yet again, spending the next little while feeling my way towards the light.

Chapter 15

The last thing I wanted was to become the girl that everybody pitied. I never indulged in self-pity, so I detested any form of sympathy from others. What I loathed more than people feeling sorry for me was being so miserably affected by someone who obviously wasn't worthy of my love. I felt furious with myself for having the ridiculous expectation that any guy could be faithful to me, because apart from Mitchell, my first, not one had been.

My co-workers all offered to take me out. They were the only people I could trust at that point, so rather than continuing to alienate those who *were* reaching out to me, even though their remedies involved copious amounts of alcohol and rebound sex, I agreed. I finally felt it was time to move on. I needed to shake off the hurt and stop hiding from the world.

Within a few weeks, I had been integrated into new social groups and made fast friendships. One older couple particularly took a shine to me. They would continually offer to buy me drinks and invite me back to their place for parties. I declined most of the time, but the one time I accepted, I ended up being the only one in attendance.

I didn't realize they were swingers. It didn't even cross my mind, and I was oblivious to the signs. Being invited back to their place didn't seem that odd. People in Australia partied all the time, so it didn't even occur to me that I might be their only guest. I remained clueless right up until that dreadful ah-ha moment when he tried to kiss me.

When they put on the porn movie, I was far too embarrassed to watch it or even comment. And when they repeatedly offered me alcohol—which I declined—I still didn't catch on. When they dragged me upstairs to "look at their new bedroom furnishings," I thought it was odd, but I was still clueless until he tried to kiss me, and she even encouraged it. She said she wanted to watch me "satisfy" her husband. Everything about that felt wrong to me.

"Stop! Nope, not interested, thanks!" I cried out. Besides the fact that they were both quite unappealing to me, I was not willing to let myself be used in their kinky sex games.

It angered me afterwards that I was never consulted beforehand, never told up front what their intentions were. I was very annoyed that my trust had been betrayed again. I raced out of their apartment as if running from a house fire, and I drove off so shaken by the ordeal that I didn't notice I was driving in the wrong direction. I had soon become lost out on a lonely, winding bush road in the middle of the night.

When I did finally reach home, it was almost dawn. I was still trembling. I climbed into bed exhausted yet unable to sleep from the night's events. I went over every detail of the evening, thinking about what signs I'd missed and what I needed to watch out for in the future. When it did, however, I was oblivious to those signs as well.

I was offered more threesomes the following year than any other time in my life. I was in no way interested. They were too risky, much too dangerous, and I just wasn't the type who could see myself participating in any form of sex act just for the hell of it. I wanted the love and passion of one person, that to me was a much bigger turn on than being banged by some sleazy dudes in a cheap room somewhere.

Once I got back on my feet, I landed myself another job and moved into another new flat with yet another new flatmate, a girl around my age. We seemed to get along well enough, so we started going out together around the coast and frequented a new bar/restaurant that had just opened up. We would go for a meal and stay to watch the band afterwards. There was finally somewhere pleasant to go out, rather than those meat-market clubs in town. Regardless, I exercised all my precautions and was wary of everybody I encountered. I still had a long way to go, however, in being able to figure out all the sly tactics for luring women into traps.

One evening, my new flatmate and I were leaving to go home when we were approached by three young men who asked us for a lift back to their place. I glanced over at her with reservations, shaking my head "No," but she was way too friendly for her own good, especially after she'd had a few. She said yes before I could protest further.

We pulled up outside their apartment and they all climbed out. I was about to pull away when they stopped us. "No, no, you girls aren't going home yet, are ya? The night's still early! Youse 'avta come up. We got beer!"

"Oh no, thanks. We're just going to go ho—"

"Okay, but just for a little while," I was interrupted by my flatmate.

Is she crazy? I could have wrung her neck!

"Just for one drink, come on. The tall one is cute!" she coerced me.

I didn't want to spoil her fun, but I worried. She virtually dragged me in. *Well, if I must. But I really don't like this.*

The minute we stepped into the elevator, they were already putting the moves on us. I managed to slip away from one but didn't have anywhere to go. When we arrived on their floor, we were ushered inside, and they headed for the fridge. They cracked open their beers and offered us some. I refused, but my friendly new flatmate accepted and almost instantly disappeared up the hall with the tall one she liked. I was shocked that she went off with a stranger so quickly. That didn't leave the situation looking too good for me. If the other two could see it was that easy, then they would assume I was just as easy.

I sat down on the sofa and arranged my clothes and position in a ladylike manner, quite annoyed that my friend had bailed on me. She left me in imminent danger. The two that were left sat down beside me, one on each side. They slid up close. My heart pounded. They came in closer, both trying to kiss me and clutching at me with their sleazy paws.

"You want to have some double fun, baby?" they breathed with their foul beer breath.

No, no, no, I don't want this. I had to find a way out quickly.

"I need to use the bathroom!" I panicked.

They pointed to where it was. Instead of following their directions, I slipped out the front door, ran out to my car and stayed there.

The next twenty minutes felt like three hours. Finally I saw my flatmate, and I was so relieved. She had her shoes in her hand, and her hair looked matted like a bird's nest. She climbed into the passenger seat with a happy kind of guilt.

"Oh, I couldn't find you. Where did you go?"

"Out here. I've been waiting for you," I answered.

"Guess we should go home now, huh?" she said, looking somewhat spent.

I guessed she had just been given a good shagging. Maybe she needed it. I didn't ask. I didn't want to get in the way of anyone's fun, but I was more than a little annoyed that I was dragged into that situation.

A few weeks after that, an old friend of mine, Shelly, invited me out to dinner with her and her male friend, who had brought along two of his buddies. She sat on one side of the table with her friend, allowing them to jabber on all evening between themselves. That left me wedged between his two mates. Neither of them appealed to me in any way, so while I maintained my good manners, I made sure I wasn't giving away any more of myself than necessary. Midway into my dessert, they ambushed me from each side, both leaning in closely.

"So are you up for some action?" the chubby one asked, raising his eyebrows.

My fork was loaded with cheesecake, so I was in no way prepared for what they had just asked.

"All you have to do is lie there. We'll do all the work!"

I scanned their faces for any glint of jest. Nothing but

raised eyebrows and anticipation.

"Are you serious?" I questioned.

"Of course! You dunno whatcha missing 'til you 'ave two at once!" the slimmer of the two added.

My eyes darted back and forth between them, aghast. They were both eagerly staring at me as if I were the lotto draw on TV. My mind raced. *That not only sounds empty and meaningless but extremely dangerous. I don't even know these bozos. They could be axe murderers for all I know. They could have anything set up at their hotel, waiting—ropes, date rape drugs, blindfolds, eighteen-inch toys, cameras, other guys waiting . . . anything. I don't think so!*

"Um . . . I . . . um, I might pass, thanks all the same," was the best brush off I could come up with on short notice. It wasn't that I was surprised by Aussie males propositioning me—that happened almost daily—but I had hoped that I could, just once, enjoy a nice dinner out with civilized people without being hit on. I thought I deserved better than that.

There were more offers that year for threesomes, but I had become a little better at seeing them coming. When two guys hung around for any length of time, I suspected what they might want. If they talked about their previous three-way experiences, I nipped them in the bud before my naivety led me into any more awkward situations. I didn't bother to take seriously the offers that were yelled out at me from passing cars.

Chapter 16

I knew Shaun wasn't right for me from the start, but he had always been pleasant to me at work, so I let my guard down a smidge. Even though he told me early on that he smoked pot, the way he nervously asked me out caught me off guard in a weak moment. I took the slim chance that all he needed was focus and a good woman like me in his life. Maybe with my influence and support, he could give up the pot and be the man he wanted to be.

That is a common mistake a lot of us women make. It wasn't the only time in my life I was going to make it either. These individuals may appear promising in the beginning, luring us with good intentions and convincing themselves, and us, that they can beat their addictions no problem. They might stop for a week or two but usually revert back to their old habits and drag us down with them. It was always the same, and this guy was no different.

It was my fault to have expected him to actually be sincere when he told me he'd love to ride a bike around France with me, hike through the Rockies or snorkel in Fiji. It was an empty promise, made only to entice me, like an introductory rate the credit card companies offer.

Every day I would discover more and more how deeply addicted to that stuff he was and what a lost cause he seemed to be. When I would bring up our loosely discussed travel plans, he displayed less and less enthusiasm as time went on.

"Yep, one day," he deflected, while leaving me to sit outside in the car for over an hour while he was scoring weed.

He thought very little about my interests, his eyes glazing over each time I talked about the ancient trees in Tasmania or the waterfalls in South America. His interests peaked at video games and packing his bong. The only time he really paid me any attention was when he made me wear the cut-off shorts and midriff-baring top he bought for me. He seemed to enjoy beating his chest with pride as he paraded me around the streets, letting me endure all the whistles and toots from passing cars. It made me feel like a cheap bit of meat, but at least *he* got to exult himself in smug, ego-boosting gratification.

It was curious that Australian males didn't seem to care if you did have male by your side. It might deter them from hurling the extremely vile stuff at you, but the honking, whistling and catcalls continued as if they weren't there. And instead of defending your honour, your boyfriend would just lap it all up with pride. I wondered if they would feel differently if it were their sister getting that attention.

When Shaun's birthday came around, I asked him where he wanted to go to celebrate. I didn't expect him to suggest a romantic, candlelight dinner, dancing or even a movie, but when I proposed a night in with pizza, beer and the footy match, I was surprised that he even turned *that* down.

The only thing he wanted to do that night was go to the Miss Nude Finals at the other end of the coast. He even wanted me to drive him there. It was being held in a pub that was often hired out for special events, and he told me that I could either wait in the car, so I could drive his drunk ass home afterwards, or I could go and sit somewhere in the back by myself. He made it clear that it was *his* night.

I knew that if I did go inside the evening wouldn't be comfortable. Experiencing Aussie blokes around *any* girls, let alone naked ones, was something I most likely wouldn't want any part of, but there was nowhere else to go in that area. Naturally, I was expecting rowdy and vile behaviour, but making unnecessary trips back and forth seemed less appealing. I decided I'd go in.

Shaun entered first. He ordered a beer from the bar and nudged his way to the front, near the stage. I entered behind him and settled myself on a chair at the back of the room. I sat near two other poor girls who didn't have much choice about being there either. We nodded to each other and simply shrugged our shoulders.

Streams of men continued to flow into the venue. The crowd bustled with males of all ages from eighteen to eighty. Some were wearing casual gear and some wore suits, obviously coming straight from their office jobs. Some were there alone and some in groups. I spotted wedding rings on many fingers, and who knows how many of them had girlfriends. Almost every one of them—I estimated about two hundred—was getting thoroughly tanked and becoming rowdy. When the lights dimmed, many swarmed the stage.

When the first girl came out, the onslaught of verbal assaults began. The other girls and I were thunderstruck over what came out of their mouths.

"Show us your c*nt, you fucking slut!"

"Eww, you're disgusting, you fucking whore!"

"Yeah, that's right, baby, show us your snatch, ya fuckin' bitch!"

"How would ya like my cock in your ass, ya slag?"

"Bend over and show us your dirty hole!"

They hooted and hollered and stomped their feet, spewing vile filth, grabbing their crotches and making lewd gestures with their tongues, genitals and hands.

A sudden searing pain speared my head as if I had been pierced by a white-hot dagger. I had heard many abhorrent remarks in my day, but not on such a large scale and never *that* bad. I became quite ill. Even the men wearing suits and the "gentleman" from older generations were just as guilty of contributing to the mass dehumanization of those poor girls.

I knew the evening wasn't about men behaving themselves; I wasn't an idiot, but it would have been nice to see *some* level of respect. These blokes seemed to think it was perfectly normal to demand to see women take off their clothes and to treat them like trash when they did. The two other girls that were sitting near me were likewise shaking their heads, unable to comprehend the level of loathsome behaviour. We were taken to a whole new level of disgust and rolled our eyes in utter bewilderment.

I felt so relieved that I had never had to take my off clothes for a living. Although being subjected to repulsive remarks, foul behaviour and constant sexual harassment was something I encountered almost every day, this was an explosion of unashamed, primal vulgarity that you couldn't pay me enough money to endure. *Do these girls actually enjoy having such obscenities hurled at them? Because I hate what I get out there on the streets, and this is so much worse.* I don't think I ever quite got over what I witnessed that evening.

My relationship with Shaun didn't last long after that, but not because of that night, or his habitual drug use or lack of ambition. Finding his porn stash didn't help things, but ultimately I had good reason to suspect that he had cheated on me or was about to.

I spotted him coming out of work one night looking very chummy with one of his co-workers. When I saw them again at the mall, smelling the fragrances that they were spraying on each other, I knew something was up. I guess it was too much to ask for a boyfriend that could be faithful. I had lost him to another, but I wasn't in love, so it was what it was. It still sucked.

* * *

The feeling of both an absence and a presence of something I couldn't quite name started haunting me just below my surface. Whatever was missing, I ached for it. I felt extremely sad and incomplete without it. Whatever was present felt like a minefield of terror bombs ready to detonate at any moment. I had to outsmart and outmanoeuvre panic attacks with every step. I felt so fragile, as if one wrong move would make them explode, taking me down the familiar path that had tortured me years ago. I had to stay positive somehow and keep ahead of the ominous danger of anxiety and depression.

The memory of that magical day, when the universe took me on that wave ride towards my happier life, was something I clung to whenever I felt myself getting too close to a panic attack. That one-minute ride was a treasured gift that I rationalized some cosmic force was responsible for. It put a 'To Be Continued" label on me instead of 'The End," and it didn't feel right to try to recapture that life-saving moment. It would only trivialize it. That was a one-time event, and I knew it. I had to find other things in my life that would give me the same energized enthusiasm if I was going to survive what I felt was coming.

My travel plans had taken another beating after continued disinterest from potential travel buddies, and not one of my friends was keen for even a nature hike. My female friends were only interested in males, and males were only interested in sex.

It was a colossal effort to keep myself feeling happy. Almost everything in my past had been sullied by violation, assault, heartbreak and misery, and any happier memories I may have had were also tarnished with something nasty.

There were only a couple of gentle things in my life that I felt warmed by, my mother and the natural world, especially animals, but they weren't quite enough. I was battling something much larger than what they could protect me from, and the threat of depression and anxiety was looming ever larger.

Chapter 17

When I wasn't in the mood to risk potential perverts approaching me on the beach, I could take solace in visiting my parents and spending time out in the grounds of their apartment complex. My spirit would often be placated by lying on a deck chair beside their deliciously refreshing, duck-friendly pool, surrounded by lush gardens. My favourite part, besides the Bird of Paradise tree, the running bamboo and little bridge that crossed the winding ponds filled with goldfish, was the rock waterfall that cascaded behind a cluster of vibrant flowers and shrubs. I could be hypnotized by it all day, feeling about as far away as I could get without actually leaving town.

My father worked his entire life so he could spend his retirement in luxurious surrounds, and despite only having a modest one-bedroom apartment, they were very happy there. It was so much easier for my mother to manage from the confines of her wheelchair.

On one of my days off from work, I was feeling quite anxious and worried that I would suffer another panic attack, so I needed a good dose of the love that my mother's company provided and the tranquil surrounds in which my parents lived.

After visiting with them for a while, I made my way down to the pool. I was lucky to be the first one there and selected my favourite spot beside the waterfall. I soon became comforted by the dancing sparkles the sun had created on the surface of the water. I fell into a soft trance of nothingness, something that was becoming harder to do.

After about ten minutes, I noticed a young boy standing outside the pool gate. He would have been no more than ten years old. I watched him as he fiddled with the lock. He didn't seem to have a key and was trying to open it by pulling and pushing on the bars as if in jail. Every resident had a key to access all the areas, so obviously his parents hadn't allowed him to have it. He just stood outside the gate a few feet away, staring at me.

I smiled at him and had a passing thought of letting him in but decided against it. If he wasn't given a key, then it would have been for a reason, and without any supervision, I didn't want to be responsible for whatever might happen. I felt sorry for him, as the crystal water would have been quite enticing for a boy his age.

"Hey lady" he called out.

As I turned around, expecting him to ask me to let him in, I witnessed him pulling his shorts aside and revealing his boyhood genitalia to me. I couldn't believe it! My eyes shot back in the other direction, and I was completely horrified. I couldn't help but wonder who had taught him to do that. I was so stunned and disturbed by what this boy did that I didn't even know how to respond. *Is it wrong for this young boy to actually make me feel violated?*

It seemed that I couldn't even enjoy peaceful surroundings once without some male ruining it for me. I was pissed off that I had actually felt sorry for this little shit of a kid only a moment ago.

He continued to stand there, hand on himself, waiting for his chance to flash me again, so I tried to ignore him, hoping he would just go away. Did his father act like that, or his brother or little warped mates? Had he seen some old creep flashing himself at women and thought "Ooh, what a great idea!"? Had he become distorted from those ridiculous ads in the back of comic books, promising X-ray glasses that would allow him to see through women's clothing? Why would these companies put that terrible idea in young boys' heads? All it did was teach them to be twisted little perverts. Were women not entitled to their privacy even from young boys? Somebody had to have been responsible for this kid's actions. This just wasn't right.

As he was still standing there, obviously waiting for me to turn around again, I lost all hope for any peace. My poolside enjoyment had been compromised. I gathered up my things and left through the opposite gate. As I went through it, I looked back to see if he was leaving also, but as I did, he flashed me again. Little shit.

I had to walk back through the foyer, so I thought I would tell management about him on the way past the reception desk. Maybe they would notify his parents, or at least go out there and tell him off.

When I approached the counter, a serious woman dressed in a navy pantsuit was busily typing at a computer. She barely acknowledged me, making me wait until she was good and ready to serve me. Her stern, unsmiling expression invited no approach, and I was made to feel like her pesky cat waiting to be let inside. After about two full minutes, she finally glanced up. She removed her eyeglasses and, with nose turning upward, she simply said, "Yes?" She reminded me of my fourth grade art teacher, who detested interruptions and any form of misbehaviour.

I took a deep breath. "Hi, I just wanted you to be aware that there is a young boy out by the pool who is flashing himself to people, well *me* actually," I reported meekly.

"Surely you're not intimidated by a young boy, are you?" she snapped at me brusquely, brow furrowed. "If you are that concerned about it, why don't you just tell him to go away?"

I couldn't believe her attitude.

"Well, I thought maybe his parents should at least be notified about what he's doing out there," I added, expecting her to agree, surely.

"Oh honestly!" she said acerbically. "Why don't you just ignore him if he is bothering you that much? You need to handle this yourself. We can't be interrupted by such small matters all the time," she said, sliding her eyeglasses back onto her nose and returning to her computer screen. She had now dismissed me, and I felt gagged and bound.

As I made my way back up to my parents' apartment, feeling quite confounded by her sharp response and complete lack of concern, I questioned myself. Did that sour bitch actually have a point? Should I have not let that young boy intimidate me like that? I'm not so sure anymore. But isn't that flippant attitude the reason why these males keep doing these repulsive things? If nothing is said or done and they aren't made accountable for their behaviour, then won't they just keep reoffending? If they are not corrected when they are young, then won't they grow up to do worse? I suddenly felt extremely confused.

Beside the outdoor pool, there was also an indoor, heated pool, which I often used. It would be the highlight of my week to slide into that heavenly tub of bubbly warmth, which would dissolve all my anxieties away. If I timed it right, I could usually get the place to myself.

One evening after finishing my half-hour swim and blissful, forty-minute spa—something I badly needed with my ever threatening panic and depression biting at my heels—I entered the female change room and started showering. The shower cubicle itself had a solid door, but just outside of that was a large, frosted window. On the other side was a small garden. I had seen that garden from the outside each time I entered that part of the building. I thought many times that if someone wanted to get in there, they would have to really squeeze themselves through the thick arrangement of dense plants and shrubs.

After I showered and towelled myself dry, I started dressing in the adjacent change area of the cubicle. That was when I heard something, a rustling sound, and it seemed to be coming from outside in that garden.

I finished dressing, slipped on my sandals and stepped out of the recess. My eyes flew immediately to a dark figure standing pressed right up against the frosted window. My first reaction was a horrified shock. My muscles tensed with a familiar sinking feeling. My mind raced instantly back to my bedroom when I saw my neighbour at my window. I felt violated all over again.

The frosted coating on the window was light enough that it allowed me to make out the shape. It was definitely a male, and he was doing something to himself. I looked closer. "Oh my!" I gasped. *He is masturbating!* At that moment, I was uncertain whether my reaction was actually audible. *What a stupid window to put in a women's bathroom!*

The male figure must have caught on that I had seen him, for in what must have been his moment of panic, he zipped up his pants and retreated back through the thick garden, bolting off up the pathway. He was gone in mere seconds.

I immediately thought I should inform management, but then remembered the reception I got last time. I didn't fancy my chances of Ms. Bitchy Pants wanting to do anything about it. Even though I was shaken by not only the violation but also the knowledge that there was a pervert running around in my parent's building, I couldn't face her. I imagined her challenging gaze, filling me with ridicule and self-doubt. I couldn't go through that again.

As I made my way up to my parent's apartment, I remembered what a girl from work had once told me. She was on a bus travelling across Australia on her own when she noticed the man in the seat opposite playing with himself. He was vigorously going at it while fixing his gaze upon her. Without hesitation, she went up and told the driver, who immediately stopped the bus. He wasn't concerned that they were smack in the middle of the outback, miles from the next small town, he chucked him off with his bag and told the dirty old wanker that he wouldn't tolerate that kind of behaviour on his bus. That was the kind of support I so desperately needed. That bus driver will forever be my hero.

* * *

I was given the news by my roommate that I had to move again. The flat we were living in had been sold, and new owners wanted us out to do renovations. After that, they'd be raising the rent. It was the same old story. I had to live with my bags permanently packed, not getting too attached to any place or any person that I shared with. It cost me a great deal of time, money and stress to be always moving. I was fed up driving all over the coast looking for places, wasting petrol, and forking out cash for hiring moving vans and disconnecting and reconnecting the utilities. Added to that was the stress and pressure of trying to evaluate, in five minutes, whether I'd get along with my potential new flatmates and then having to fit into new dynamics and house rules.

Sharing sucked. I had to continually learn new personality types, put up with their friends, their quirks, their schedules, their music, their pantyhose hanging from the curtain rail, their wet towels on the floor, their dramas and their dirty dishes. Then there were the endless debates and arguments over bills, cleaning schedules, what stuff we could and couldn't use, missing food and who exactly was it that put a scratch on the coffee table.

I was exasperated by the prospect of going through all that yet again, so I thought if I leased my own place, I could at least have more say over what went on. I could also be more selective over who I shared with.

After weeks of searching, I finally settled on a place I liked. Shortly after unpacking and setting it up the way I liked, I advertised for a flatmate. It was a time before the Internet and any form of social media, so the only option was to take ads out in the classified section of the newspapers. Cellphones hadn't become mainstream quite yet, so every residence needed a landline phone or nobody could contact you. My mistake was to write in the ad "Flatmate needed to share with single female."

The calls started coming in immediately. Almost every caller was male.

"So ya got'nee room for a coupla dogs?"

"Got'neething against pot?"

"How d'ya feel about someone practisin' the sax?"

"Do ya like to party?"

"Maybe we could do some lines together." *I'm sure that didn't mean rehearsing a script.*

On the fourth day, those calls were all trumped by one I received late in the afternoon.

"Oh, so you are there by yourself, are ya? You want me to come over and give ya a good time? *How did he know I was alone? Oh right the ad, stupid, stupid.* "If y'are there alone, then how about I come ova and give you whatcha need? I got a big cock for ya darlin'. You'd really enjoy yourself. You'd want that, wouldn't ya?"

I slammed down the phone then quickly dashed about the place, locking every window and door, now terrified of being there alone. The repercussions of writing "single female" in my ad hadn't even occurred to me. The phone rang again immediately, but I didn't answer.

I ended up choosing the only girl who applied, Chloe. She was from Yugoslavia and worked in town at an Italian restaurant. She came crashing into my life like a whirlwind. I actually quite enjoyed her exuberance and her loud, peculiar personality. I needed someone like that around to keep me from slipping into another depression.

She was awesome to walk anywhere with too. The moment any guys would yell something out from their cars, she'd give it right back to them. One young driver called out, "Suck my cock bitches!"

Chloe's response was classic. "In your dreams, little dick!" she retorted, wiggling her pinky finger.

The carload of young men erupted into cheers, followed by teasing banter, ribbing their mate and making him look like a complete fool. I couldn't believe it. It was brilliant!

On another day, another car tooted, and the driver yelled, "You'se girls lookin' for a root?" I had to translate for her that *root* meant *sex*.

"Yeah", she yelled back, "do you know anyone good

looking that can outlast and outperform you?”

Again, the car erupted into cheers and applause as the blokes mocked their buddy. It was absolutely hilarious! I’d never seen anyone do that before.

To me, her words were lyrical and poetic, executed perfectly, because for the first time I felt that justice was finally being served. I witnessed first-hand those young guys being outsmarted, and I had myself another hero. I wanted to try it myself, but the shackles of fear were locked far too tightly. It was going to take me a lot of convincing, and possibly a whole new personality, to actually muster up the courage. I promised myself that one day I would, if I ever felt brave enough.

Chapter 18

Sitting upon the cool sand, breathing in the night sea air still wasn't enough to make me feel any better. My head continued to swirl, and that horrid, *not-all-there* feeling made me feel woozy and faint. Being teased about my drug-induced state by the rough-talking dope addict sitting next to me was making it so much worse. He had been pestering me all night, and I just wished he would just go away and leave me the hell alone. I needed desperately to lie down.

I didn't invite him to sit on the beach with me, nor did I ask him to take me away from my new friends at the cafe and hound me all night until I could score some dope for him. When I finally did get to return to the café, Chloe and her girlfriends had left. Because I was gone for so long, they probably assumed I wasn't coming back. Little did she know that this "pest friend" of her friend, who earlier approached our table to say hello, had been holding me hostage while he "tested the product" that he had forced me into finding for him.

The last thing I wanted to do that night was to be forced into leaving my new friends to take some aggressive, low-life, desperate addict around to my ex's place so he could score some weed. I also didn't want to be made to sit for almost an hour with a bunch of wacked out potheads while becoming increasingly ill and trippy from second-hand ganja smoke.

Why did I say it? When someone asks me, "Do you know anyone with some smoke?" Just say "No" straight up, not "Maybe". What an idiotic thing to say. God I'm so stupid sometimes. I just hadn't expected the guy to stand over me like he did after I said it. He wasn't going to let me go until I followed through. I also didn't expect to then be actually involved in a two-bit drug deal.

His stand-over tactics worked. This feral-looking ruffian practically bullied me into calling this "maybe" connection for him, and the only person I could think of who lived nearby and could possibly have some was my ex, Shaun. After having an extremely awkward conversation on the phone with the guy who preferred dope, strippers, porn and other girls to me, I walked this wild-eyed guy over to his place. The entire way there, I worried about whether or not I was going to be attacked, but, at that point, he was more interested in buying drugs than he was in me.

Once I led him right to the door and introduced them, I thought that was it, and my part was over. I was expecting to be left to return to my friends at the café where I should have stayed, where I should have just shut up and not tried to joke with a stranger. Apparently, that wasn't going to happen just yet. I was told to go inside and wait while the deal went down and to sit on a ripped vinyl sofa while the two of them and the flatmate all passed around the dirty, stinking bong. The plumes of bushfire-smelling smoke were so thick and suffocating that the room started spinning, and I felt like I was on an out-of-control Ferris wheel ride. That stuff made me so loopy that I hardly remembered the walk back into town.

When I finally did get back to where this awful night all began, my heart sank when I saw Chloe and her friends were gone. What was worse, I still couldn't get rid of this guy and his "escort service" bit was growing very old. He was now in a different mood than he had been earlier, much chattier and less aggressive, but still roughly spoken and someone I just wanted to get away from. My head was spinning so much I had to rest somewhere before I fell down.

"I'm just going to go sit down at the beach for a bit," I explained, taking myself off towards the boardwalk, hoping that would finally be the end of him.

"Great I'll come with ya!" he announced, in the same way that young guy had said on the ship before he followed me to my cabin and pounced on me. His words sent an angry chill rushing through my body, but without a backup plan and a desperate need for that fresh sea breeze and the cool sand, I didn't feel I had any choice about the matter. It was just the way my night had been going.

As we stepped onto the sand, I noticed a few people playing about, joking and laughing by the water's edge and silvery light from the wave crest rising and crashing upon the shore. I wanted to plop down right where I first stood, safely illuminated by the lamps on the boardwalk, but he suggested we go a little farther, into the shadows and out of earshot of anybody that was about.

We both plopped ourselves down. He laughed and mocked me, mumbling something about being an "amateur," which annoyed me mightily, making me want to smash his face in, not that I would have or could have. So I let myself fall backwards instead. I was hoping that by lying on my back, I could fixate my eyes upon the stars, and it would stop my head from spinning. That was the plan anyway, a nice, simple plan that I could relax into.

I started to concentrate on one bright star and the soft glow that surrounded it, praying to it, silently asking for an end to this out-of-control feeling I detested so supremely. This is why I never allowed myself to get drunk or high. I hated the effects. I loathed not being in control of myself and detested being on this horrid ride of light-headed, spinning wooziness. This was the worst I had felt in a very long time.

Being in that horizontal position, looking up at the stars, I didn't notice this guy had undone the zipper on his jeans, nor did I see him coming in on me. His legs came into view first. He positioned them one each side of me, straddling me, now sitting on my chest with his dick coming into full view. He had worked himself up to an erection, and before I had time to process what was now suddenly happening, he stuffed it into my mouth. I was in no way prepared. Five seconds ago, I was staring at stars, and now I had some grubby fucker's cock in my mouth.

He started thrusting it ferociously, in and out, in and out, holding my head in place while he pleasured himself. My mouth was so deprived of saliva since becoming affected by all that dope earlier that it felt like I was having a dry, stale hotdog brutally shoved down in there, causing me not only fear of not being able to breath, but also of vomiting. He rhythmically pushed and shoved in and out with forceful movements, and I could feel the blood draining away from my face and head. The only thing I seemed to have control over was to try to close off the back of my throat so he couldn't reach my gag reflex trigger. I wanted to bite down, to cause him real serious harm, but his fierce prodding was pushing my lips in the way of my teeth.

I recall grabbing at his legs, trying to pry him off but being completely overpowered and trapped. All I could do was wait until he was finished with me. This continued for what seemed to be around three minutes, but I wasn't sure in reality how long it actually was, perhaps somewhere between one and two. It felt longer.

I was too faint and dizzy to experience the horrified, sobering terror I otherwise would have, had I not been so out of it, but what I did feel was shock, surprise, revolt, disgust and violation. He removed himself completely from my mouth and didn't thrust it back in. I was unaware of what was going on. *Is it over? Is he done?* I couldn't tell what was happening; I couldn't see what he was doing. He removed his legs from around me and rolled off onto the sand beside me. *I think he must be done.*

This was my opportunity to get away. I somehow managed to scramble to my feet and took off running without another thought, back across the sand and up towards the steps. I finally made it onto the boardwalk and didn't look back. I had parked my car earlier that night along the beach a few blocks away, so I sprinted to where I remembered it was. As I ran, I felt something wet and sticky in my hair. I raised my hand up to feel what it was, worried that it may have been blood, but I didn't see any red, only a sticky white substance. I felt vomit rising into my throat, but I kept running.

Once I finally reached the safety of my car, I climbed in and shut the door fast. I glanced at myself in the rear-view mirror and could see how ruined I looked. I straightened myself a little, trying to wipe the sticky goo from my hairline, but had no tissues or anything in my vehicle I could use. I needed to stop my hands from shaking, so I took a few deeply controlled breaths and talked calmly to myself. I had to try to get my head together so I could drive home. That was the last thing I should have done in the state I was in, but I wanted to get the hell away from there as fast as I could.

The drive home was a complete blur, however, I did recall seeing a police car and ambulance van when I pulled up at home. They were parked in the driveway next door, and our young neighbour was being taken away. This was a common scene. He was a heroin addict who routinely caused trouble in the neighbourhood, having overdosed on a number of occasions. I had to try to slip inside before they nabbed me for driving home while under the influence.

I didn't even think to report to them what had just taken place. I was scared, still feeling very loopy and confused about whether that was actually worth reporting. *Was that considered rape?* If I had taken some time in my life to inform myself about all these sex crimes that were being committed against me, I could have had him—him and so many more before him. When was I going to learn that it was only up to me, that nobody was going to tell me what I needed to know, what I needed to do and that these were reportable crimes? *Stupid, stupid.* I needed to crash.

* * *

As the sunlight broke through the darkness and streamed in through my bedroom window, I awoke to the memory of what had happened, yet I felt more numb than angry. I may not have been emotionally or mentally ready to face what horrors might be heading my way in the next few hours, days, weeks or months. Perhaps I was simply anesthetized or shutting down emotionally, but right then, while I lay warm and comfortable, focusing only on the sounds of the warbling of the morning magpies, I put the scene in the back of my mind and concentrated on my day ahead.

I had a five-hour day shift at my new office job, and I also had a three-hour shift later at the cinema where I had picked up a bit of extra work. They both were only part-time, and even though they taxed me heavily for my second job, I couldn't survive with just one, so I simply didn't have any choice.

Despite not feeling anywhere near my normal self at either of my jobs that day—and many people had noticed—I didn't reveal anything of what happened. I just felt too ashamed. I lied about not feeling well and kept my head down, trying to go unnoticed.

I worked at both jobs the next day, then the next, and all the rest of that week, then all of the next. I remained dazed and dull, keeping the memories of that night off in the distant place so it couldn't hurt me for a while.

After I finished my shift at the cinema at the end of that fortnight, I walked out to my car that I had parked out on the street. To make myself feel safer, I always made sure I parked right outside the complex in the main shopping area under the lights in the busiest section of the street.

I slipped into the driver's seat and pulled out on the road to head for home. Just as I did, the car parked two car lengths away pulled out as well. He followed me all the way down to the end of the main street. By the time I reached the end, I turned left, and so did he. I didn't worry too much at that point, as *that* road was still one of the main streets, but I did notice that he was following me rather closely.

We continued down for a few minutes, and, as it was a two-lane road, I was expecting him to overtake me. He didn't. He stayed right behind my tail. I then turned off into a side street, one of the smaller, quieter suburban roads I needed to take to get home. Sure enough, he turned too. That was when I became worried.

At the end of that road, I turned again, then again. He was still only a few feet behind. I tensed all my muscles and looked back into my rear-view mirror to see who I was dealing with. What I could make out was a dimly lit male face, probably around sixty years old and wearing a baseball cap. I would imagine he was trying to conceal himself, because I couldn't see his face clearly. As he caught me looking at him, the corner of his mouth turned upwards, and he smirked in that same kind of lecherous sneer I had seen so many times before. I knew at that moment that this man was playing some sick game.

Searing heat rushed from the bottom of my spine to the base of my neck in an instant, and my mind started to spin faster than what I could keep up with. Every emotion that had been lying dormant from the night at the beach only two weeks earlier surged through my body at once, filling me with an explosion of horrific fear and angry adrenalin. I was now in a full-blown panic.

What the hell does he want from me? What the hell am I going to do? There's no cop station for miles. My only thoughts were about getting home, as it felt like the safest option. The car continued to follow directly behind me the entire way, mimicking my every turn, my every movement, right up until I arrived home. That's when he started playing even more games.

The house I was renting was on a corner of a through road and a cul-de-sac, which he used to turn his car around and continue to taunt me. I pulled up into my driveway and just sat there, too petrified to move. He crawled past me slowly, glaring and staring at me on the way. When he reached the end of the street, he turned around again, inching past, trying to meet my eyes. In the rear mirror, I saw that smirk again. I knew that grin well. It belonged to people with twisted, dark souls who I would encounter when I least expected to.

I sat as rigid as a board for at least three full minutes, trapped in my terror, tormented as if being circled by a twenty-foot man-eater. I couldn't help but think that there must be something about me that predators pick up on, but I had no idea what they saw. Perhaps they sensed my fear. I remained in my vehicle, tortured and praying for a saviour, feeling a critical sense of dread. *Have I not been tortured enough?*

That very second, Chloe appeared in the doorway and started down the stairs. Trailing behind her was a male friend of hers, whom she was saying goodbye to. She waved at me and continued talking to her friend. They didn't notice my predicament. The second their feet touched the bottom of the stairs, my stalker took off with a screeching roar up the street. Chloe and her friend looked up. He was gone in seconds.

Twenty minutes later, while trying to soak my ordeal away in my Juniper and Thyme bath of bubbles, it struck me suddenly and soberly. I didn't even think to get a clear description of that guy or his car. I didn't get his license plate number or any identifying features I could have used to report that creep. *Was that considered stalking? Could I have reported him?* Of course it was. Why did I not know these things?

When he was following me earlier, I did plan to call the police when I got home—but only if he refused to leave or threatened me further. It didn't occur to me that if I had gathered enough information, I still could have made one simple phone call and potentially stopped that man from stalking, following, and terrorizing other women. *I've just let that guy away scot-free!*

I felt a mighty disappointment in myself. I had just set up goodness knows how many other poor, unsuspecting females out there who could be his next victim because I didn't think rationally and didn't make him accountable for his crime. I needed to get out from under this crippling fear, if not for me, then for the sake of all those other girls and women who were going to be victimized by those who I didn't report.

To all those women who may have suffered from the actions of any of these men in my stories, I truly apologize and am sorry I didn't know what to do to stop them.

Chapter 19

It was a sultry summer evening around half past ten when I drove into town and started looking for somewhere to park. I was to meet Chloe and some of her workmates after they finished their shift at the restaurant. Apparently she wanted me to meet her co-worker, an Italian man a little older than me, who I was told had a gentle personality and was someone she thought I would hit it off with. I was now almost thirty and thinking maybe a European man might be better for me.

A parking spot opened up on the side of the road, the front space of three, so I pulled over in front of it and carefully backed in. There were two young males sitting in a utility truck—or *ute* as we call them—behind me in the middle space. I immediately braced myself, noticing that they looked to be the typical type to harass women and act like idiots.

When I turned off the engine and hopped out of my car, the driver called out of his window, "If you don't move it, lady, I'm gunna ram ya!" His tone sounded somewhat serious, but not enough to convince me that he wasn't actually joking. It certainly wasn't what I was expecting.

I assessed how I had parked and saw absolutely nothing wrong, in fact it was the most perfect parking job I had done in quite a while, well within the markings and well spaced both front and back. I had only recently bought a second-hand, compact-sized hatchback, so there was more than enough room for this guy to pull out safely on to the road. I looked at him, shrugged my shoulders and tried to assure him that he had plenty of room.

"I'm not kiddin'. If ya don't move it, I'm gunna ram ya!" he said. He not only sounded aggressive this time, but downright rude. It seemed he wanted to be a jerk, just for the sake of being a jerk. From his slurred speech and flushed cheeks, it was evident they'd been drinking and shouldn't have been trying to operate a vehicle in the first place. From the filthy state of his ute, their shabby clothes and tough-talking, cocky attitude, they had most likely struck out with some girls earlier, so they had to get back at someone. I didn't really care. I just wanted to get on with my evening in peace.

He started revving his engine, warning me that my little car was no match for his grunting beast and that it was about to meet its doom. In the hope that his mate might be more reasonable, my eyes flew to his, and I searched for any tiny glint of mercy. I was crushed with disappointment when he mouthed the words, "You'd better move!" My hesitation must have pushed him to the edge.

"Okay, you asked for it. I told ya!" he hollered. With that, he rammed my car with his mighty truck, pushing it an entire car length forward. He then pulled out on the road, slammed his truck into reverse and screeched backwards the entire length of the main road before dozens of onlookers and me, in cold shock and disbelief! *What the hell?*

I assessed the damage to my little hatchback, and quite surprisingly, the impact hadn't done too much harm. There were only a few minimal scratches. Nonetheless, I was pissed off. If I hadn't promised to meet Chloe and her friends, I would have given up and driven home right then, but I had told her I was coming, so I didn't want her to worry. I climbed back into my little car and reversed it into the space once again, slowly breathing my way through my shaken, anxiety-filled ordeal.

Why didn't I get his plate number and report those guys? Stupid, stupid. Without their plate number, my efforts would have been futile. *Think next time. Think!*

I needed something familiar and comforting. I arrived to meet Chloe just as she and her friends were heading over to the bar. She introduced me to Antonio, who seemed quite nice initially. He was quite thin, dark and not someone I would normally go for, but pleasant all the same. I liked that he was softly spoken and appeared to have manners.

Unfortunately, I wasn't in the best of moods. After what had just happened, I couldn't quite muster enough effort to be pleasant company for very long. I also hated being in town. I detested the clubs and had wanted to avoid that whole area as much as possible.

Around midnight, I decided to leave. Antonio equally hated the whole bar scene and asked if he could escort me back to my car.

"Maybe another time," I replied. I liked him, but didn't want to feel as if we were on a date.

"Sure, maybe you would like to go for a drink somewhere quieter next time?" he asked. He was smiling and being friendly without being pushy. I liked that. It was as if he was saying, "If you want to that's cool, if not then no problem." He gave me room to breathe, and I appreciated it.

"Absolutely," I replied.

As I made my way back along the streets, I recorded certain scenes in my mind as I passed them by. I witnessed four young blokes outside one club who were involved in a punch up over goodness knows what, probably a girl. One had lost his shoes. *Ah good ol' Surfers Paradise, a poetic paradise ruined by alcohol-fuelled violence and aggression.*

I then saw two girls in very short skirts and too high stilettos. One was hunched on the pavement throwing up on the base of a palm tree; the other was trying to keep her hair from falling in the vomit puddle. Both were being observed by two guys who looked like they were waiting to take advantage of them. *I hope they get themselves into a taxi soon and go home where they'll be safe.*

A few steps farther, I mentally snapped a picture of a sour-faced, lumbering bouncer holding some guy up by his throat against a club wall. He passed out. The beefy door guard simply let him collapse to the ground. *Crikey!*

"Nice ass, baby. How much?" a voice called out from behind me.

I whipped around and saw a couple of guys walking

closely behind me. They had that rude, arrogant, cocky look all of them seemed to have, with a smug, self-assured, boorish attitude to match. I said nothing, turned back around and dashed off ahead, back towards my poor, bruised, little car. I drove out of there wondering whether I'd ever be treated decently in this life.

* * *

At the first sign of daybreak, I leapt out of bed in a full-blown panic attack. I was thunderstruck with the realization that everything in my future looked cold, empty and inordinately bleak. It was dreadful. I desperately searched in my mind for anything to pull me out of it, anything I could feel positive or happy about, but I could only find blackness.

It took every last modicum I could muster from deep within my core to work my way through the attack. Panic is an extremely powerful force to try to negotiate with, and when I finally did manage to crawl from underneath its terrorizing clutches, I felt completely shattered.

Something had to change. I had to overcome this anxiety somehow. I needed a concrete plan for my future, but everything I wanted for myself seemed so out of reach. Each time I tried to head towards something, I would be evicted from my home, given even fewer hours at work, cheated on by a boyfriend or faced with car trouble, leaving me with an empty bank account.

Continually being treated poorly by males didn't help either. They would take a little piece away from me each and every time, leaving me to struggle to believe in myself. That was almost impossible to do when I had very little to go on, but I just had to try to continue on.

The following day, I was told I had to move again. Yet another landlord wanted to sell up, saddling me with another disruption of my life and another move. When I delivered the news to Chloe, she actually took it well and had lined up another place to go within a few hours. It was sad that she was leaving, and we had decided to part ways. I really did enjoy her cheerfulness, and she certainly was a true master at making me smile when I really needed it.

In a few weeks, I found another share apartment with another female. I didn't get too attached to the place or to her, because nothing in my life ever lasted long enough to form any bonds.

The day after I moved into my new flat, my car broke down. I knew it wouldn't be long before I realized I was sold another piece of junk. This time, it was the CV joints that needed repair. It was possibly the result of my car being shoved by those angry boys in their ute a few weeks back, but I couldn't be certain. My new flatmate was good enough to drive me back and forth to the mechanic.

While I was paying the huge repair bill at the counter, a young apprentice came out to the reception area. He looked to be around thirty with a mop of messy hair and outfitted in stained overalls and steel-toed work boots. After wiping the oily muck from his hands onto the already blackened rag that drooped out from his pocket, he studied my repair form on the counter. I was expecting him to talk to me about the repair or why it cost so much, so I was surprised by what he actually said next.

"Oh, so you live in those units on Market Street do ya? Which numba?" he asked impudently.

Why does he want to know that? Isn't he going to tell me about my car?

"Um, yes, I live just near the shops there," I deflected, hoping we could get back on track.

"Yeah, I know that apartment building. What numba is yours?" he pressed.

My gut churned. There was no way I was going to give some grubby stranger my personal information whether he had worked on my car or not.

"Oh, mine is near the shops. I live with another girl," I

answered, feeling stuck. My head began swimming, trying to work out why he wanted to know.

"Yeah but *where* exactly? Which unit?" he persisted. I was unconvinced that his attempt at a harmless-looking smirk deserved my trust. I didn't trust that smirk, I knew it too well, and it usually meant trouble for me.

What is he planning to do? Is he going to come over in the middle of the night and rape me? My face flushed with the anxiety I could feel rising up. I wanted so badly to scream out, "Get lost and mind your own business, you ugly jerk," but I was a lady. I was also now scared.

"I um, well I'm not sure exactly. I only just moved in," I spluttered, stalling for time.

"So are you gunna tell me or what?" he almost barked, still expecting me to fall for his innocent smirk.

I could feel the temperature of my blood heating within my veins. The receptionist wasn't doing much to help me and seemed as perplexed as I was by his obstinate determination. She tried questioning him with a look, but he was paying her no mind.

I needed out, and I needed it that second. I grabbed my receipt and fled for the door. When I spotted my car, I ran over and slipped into it, fast. I took off like a bat out of hell. My hands shook, and I felt completely rattled. *What was that all about? Do I now have to add to this my list of worries? Do I have to now deal with another menacing threat to my sanctity and peace of mind?*

I daydreamed about a fantasy world where males had no sexual desires or egos. How wonderful *that* place would be. In my mind, so battered by abuse, that meant there would be no wars, no woman or child would ever be hurt, and neither tears nor blood would ever be shed. I liked the sound of that.

Chapter 20

Antonio called. He asked me if it was okay that Chloe had given him my new number. I knew she was trying to pair the two of us up, so I was fine with it.

"No problem, if you turn out to be an axe murderer, I'll blame her!"

We shared a laugh, and he asked me out. I met him for a quiet drink, and we hit it off. Before long, we were in a relationship, which lasted for the next three years. I thought I was happy, and I guess I was for a while.

Being Italian, he was far removed from anything typically Australian, so naturally I found that alluring. I became drawn to everything that was different about him. I also liked his compatriots, at first anyway.

His co-workers, associates and friends might not have been lewd, crude or sexist like so many Aussie men, but over time, I was saddened to discover they were a long way from being able to take any moral high ground over anyone. It was shocking how disloyal they were. In fact, they were the most unfaithful, sex-crazed, deceptive, untrustworthy bunch of cheating rats I'd ever met!

Over the duration of our three-year relationship, Antonio's closest friend frequently made moves on me, as did his boss and his seventy-year-old father. Many of his co-workers and regular customers frequently hit on me and every other girl they fancied, whether they were in a relationship or not. Husbands were being unfaithful; boyfriends were always on the prowl; and all their women would complain. It was staggering how much of it was going on. It actually made me quite ill. Up until that time, I had hoped that Europeans were a better class of males, but sadly, they proved me wrong.

Antonio and I started having issues, many of them. Some were his; some were mine, and the stress of trying to deal with them all brought on another horrendous chapter of prolonged anxiety. Every day, more than once a day, I was caught up in a maelstrom of heart-pounding, frenzied panic. Not only was I tormented by the attacks, but I also had a constant feeling of being crushed. It felt as though a tremendous weight were sitting on my chest, leaving me unable to breathe.

It was becoming more and more difficult to hide it from Antonio, and he found me one day, slumped on the front stoop, trembling and unable to rise. I could no longer keep up the illusion of happiness and had to be honest with both him and myself.

Sadly, we came to an end. I just didn't have the strength to deal with the enormity of our problems another day. It was an extremely difficult decision to part ways, but the honest truth was, as much as I wanted to be, I wasn't in love with the man. We had nothing in common. Less than nothing. I cared for him deeply and felt a great fondness towards him, but it wasn't enough. I didn't feel what I needed to feel for him, and in my heart I was left yearning for something so much more. I wasn't certain if I could find it or not, but I owed it to myself to try. Didn't I?

* * *

Over the next year or two, I worked in a high-end department store. Every day I tried to meet my ridiculously high sales budgets, by selling overpriced goods to people who didn't need them, while my high-heeled feet snarled at me.

During one of my shifts in the accessories department, while adjusting my display of Ray-Bans, my friend Nichole's boyfriend came in. Nichole and I had once worked together, and I still considered her a friend. Her boyfriend, Daniel, approached me and said hello.

Our brief chat was pleasant and mostly about our mutual friend, both agreeing how lovely she was. His extended grin and enthusiastic nodding while declaring his love for her lulled me into a false sense of security. He fooled me into thinking he was actually devoted to her, so I recoiled in surprise when he suddenly advanced upon me.

There was no warning. I had no reason to suspect he was being disingenuous, so when he slipped in behind me and pressed his groin against my behind, a shudder ran up my spine and I froze, stupefied. *Is he for real?*

He moved his hands around to the front of my body, one hand grabbing at my breast, the other moving down towards my crotch. "Mmm, nice!" he whispered.

I was completely confounded by his disloyalty. This was so wrong on so many levels!

I quickly scanned the floor, looking for anyone who might have been a witness to what was happening, but I couldn't spot a single soul. There were no other staff and not one lousy customer in my entire department. At that moment, right when I needed someone to be around, the store had become freakishly deserted. I am fairly certain that he must have noticed this, giving him his window of opportunity. I grabbed his hands, stopping him from touching me.

"Ah come on. Ya know just 'cause I'm with Nikki, doesn't mean I can't explore!" he whispered in my ear, convinced that I had wanted this.

The nerve of this wanker, with the one hand he declares his love for his girlfriend, and with the other he is grabbing at me. How can a person possibly love someone and touch another? I will never understand this level of betrayal. Never, ever!

"Get off, Daniel!" I wriggled out of his hold. I wanted him to get the message without enraging him. There was nobody around to help me in case he snapped.

"Oh, nice. What a friend *you* turned out to be!" he retaliated with a pathetic attempt to lay blame on me. Bruised male egos always seemed to stoop to that level. When he turned to leave, I wanted to yell out profanities I would never normally speak, but I crumbled in fear of setting him off and perhaps making things worse. *If I could only be as brave as my friend Chloe. She wouldn't have hesitated.*

I returned to my duties, head shaking and with a familiar gamut of unwanted emotions—violation, shock, disgust and anger. And once again, I faced the added dilemma of whether to tell my friend that her boyfriend was a cheating rat.

My quandary was interrupted by the approach of a customer, an older gentleman. *Great* now *somebody comes!* He looked to be around sixty, wearing your run-of-the-mill clothing for our warm climate: shorts, T-shirt and sandals. He asked me the whereabouts of the women's swimwear department. It was a little hard to explain, so given how quiet the store was, I decided to lead him over there.

"Over here, Sir," I guided professionally. He trailed after me. "Here it is, Sir, I hope you find what you are looking for," I said tunefully.

"Thanks a bunch, lady. Just one thing though?" he asked.

"Sure, how can I help?"

"Do ya reckon you could try on these?" he asked, grabbing a random bikini off the rack. His eyes scanned up and down my body. "I reckon you're a pretty good sort, so you'd look great in these, waddya reckon?" he winked.

"No, sorry!" I blurted with surprising intensity, my heart pounding. "No, I'm sorry," I dialled my volume down, "I can't do that, Sir. I have to get back." *What do I look like, your private bikini model you dirty old pervert?*

Hot blood pumped through my veins. I was still reeling from Daniel's grabby hands and now this! I imagined popping that old geezer right in the kisser, but I had to remain professional.

It was a popular and busy store, so over the days, weeks and months, I ran into many people I knew, including an old friend of my brother's, Andrew. He noticed me stocking some jewellery on the counter stands and decided to come over to say hello. His buddy was with him, so when he said hi, I expected him to introduce us. He never did though, making our conversation a tad awkward. Andrew looked about the store. "So this where you work, huh?"

"Uh-huh," I nodded.

He became curiously captivated by the private beauty-therapy rooms only a few feet away.

"What are they for?" he asked, pointing at them.

"Oh, they are the beauty rooms we use for facials and skin treatments and such," I answered smiling.

"Hmm," he smirked, "so can I get a treatment from *you*?" he asked raising his right eyebrow. I recoiled in a secret mortification.

"Oh no, they are only for the ladies who have booked in for private facials, pedicures, massages, that type of thing," I replied, doing what I could to deflect him.

"Oh, *private* rooms 'ey? How about you book me in and you can give me a special treatment. Surely you can *fit me in*!" he smirked again. He obviously thought he was being clever in front of his mate.

His inappropriate suggestion caused me to instantly loath him. What I detested more than being sexually harassed was being hit on while I was working. I didn't justify it with a response.

"Oh, come on. Let's just you and me go in. Don't worry about gettin' caught," he pressed further.

He was a nice-looking, fit young man with striking green eyes and a gorgeous smile, I'll give him that, but I had no interest in being sexual with anyone who approached me in such a way, whether they were hot or not. I deserved better. I couldn't believe I had to even respond to such a ridiculous offer.

"No sorry, I can't do that Andrew. I'm working, and I *would* get caught, and I could lose my job!"

"Oh come on. Nah, ya won't get caught if we close the door. Come on. It'll be fun!" he persisted.

His words pushed their way into my personal space,

shattering any respect I might have once had for him as my brother's friend. I hadn't seen this guy in years, and he just turned up out of the blue, pressuring me for sex? *I don't think so.*

"Come on. Dontcha wanna have any fun?" he persevered.

I felt further strong-armed by the presence of his mate, who stood there smirking, most likely being thoroughly entertained by his friend's unrelenting pursuit. It was two against one. I guess I shouldn't have been so shocked by his impudence, he wasn't the first or last of my brother's mates to proposition me.

My co-worker came dashing onto the scene to fetch a customer order from the drawer next to the cash register. The interruption couldn't have come at a better time and was enough to call off the pursuit.

"So maybe some other time then," he said, backing off.

I almost collapsed with relief when they turned to leave. I exhaled slowly, desperately needing to take my tea break.

I had no idea where that had all come from. I certainly never gave that guy any indication that I was interested in him, not even once. Perhaps it wasn't me at all. Maybe it was simply society that was to blame. With all of the provocative imagery and messages out there, was that not teaching us that a woman's body is supposed to be a thing of service? It was no wonder that men expected us to conform to those beliefs.

Chapter 21

When I finally agreed to meet someone my work colleague, Wendy, had been pushing on me, she was so thrilled she practically tripped over her own words.

"Oh, he's very handsome, a real genuine guy, a hard worker!" she gushed. "And did I tell you he has his own business? He's a builder, works for himself, he does!" she bounced, clapping her hands. "Oh goodie, this is going to be great!"

If this blind date had been for just the two of us, I don't think I would have agreed, but because it was for informal drinks with a group of people at Wendy's house, the pressure was off. I said yes.

I arrived a little late, because my car wouldn't start, so there were already around ten people sitting at the kitchen table. They were all talking, laughing, drinking and nibbling on the nuts and chips that were set out in bowls. Most of the men looked like they had come straight from their trade jobs, still wearing their high visibility shirts and muddy work boots. I nodded pleasantly and smiled at everyone as Wendy did the round of introductions.

A tall, dark-haired man, wearing jeans and a slightly stained T-shirt, rose and walked towards me. *I think this is the one I am being set up with.*

"Joy, this is Travis, the one I've been telling you about," Wendy beamed, "Travis, Joy, Joy, Travis!"

"How's it goin'? Nice to meetcha!" he said, shaking my hand so much, it was as if I'd grabbed a live electrical cable. My shoulder almost popped out from the fierce jerking of my arm. His strong features were somewhat handsome, but his height and rough manner put me off a little.

I was offered a seat and a drink. I decided I'd have a small vodka and lemonade. I needed to take the edge off my nerves. It was about the third drink I had accepted in three years.

After half an hour or so, someone decided to start a drinking game. The rules were that one person had to ask someone a question, and that person would have to answer by rhyming with the question. If they could do it, and do it well, the person who asked the question had to guzzle the rest of their drink down in one go, something we call *skulling*.

The questions were all about sex, which wasn't surprising, and the answers became more vulgar as the game went around the table. The use of profanities started increasing as more drinks were skulled. I cringed at the overuse of not just the F-word, but also the C-word. *My goodness, Mum would have a stroke if she heard this stuff!*

I began feeling extremely nervous about having to ask or answer a question. I just couldn't bring myself to be that vile. My mother had raised me to be a lady, and although that drink had relaxed me a touch, I was not willing to become such a feral human being. When it was my turn, I would try to steer the game in another direction. Maybe someone would be considerate enough to answer without any smut, especially my "date."

It was now my turn to ask a question. I had mentally prepared one, so I turned and faced Travis. "Okay, what about your life are your favourite bits?" I asked, hopeful of some sign of maturity.

"Pulling out my cock and cumming over your tits!" he blurted out proudly.

The room erupted into a whooping cheer and raucous laughter, with high-fives and stomping feet. He was announced the winner of the contest. I wasn't just disappointed, but downright insulted. *Is this how someone tries to make a good first impression?*

From the delight he was taking in accepting his title, blowing on his fingernails then rubbing them on his shirt, I knew it was time to leave. I thanked Wendy for the invitation and the introduction. She completely understood that I was going.

"Sorry, I thought he'd be better behaved than this, my bad," she apologized.

"No, it's fine. I just have to get home . . . work tomorrow and all," I fibbed.

* * *

On the drive home, disheartened from another ruined night out, I passed a vegetarian café that I had been to once, years ago, when it was the only place that offered healthy eats on the coast. I have never forgotten that day.

I was invited by a then friend of mine, Mick, who was one of the first people I got to know when I moved to the coast. It took somebody to tell me he had a powerful crush on me, otherwise, in my youth and naivety, I wouldn't have caught on.

"Why do you think he is constantly hanging around and turning up at the door all the time?" my sister said, trying to drill it into me. I was slow to pick up on the signs.

While sitting in the booth, waiting for our tofu burgers, I was shoved into a shocking and highly inappropriate conversation.

"I just can't seem to stop masturbating!" my friend shamelessly confessed.

I leaned back against the booth, feeling the blood rush to my face, unsure whether to continue to wait for the food or simply bolt out the front door. Being only eighteen years of age at the time and having had only one boyfriend, I was not mature enough or ready to discuss such a thing. *Eww, is he serious? That's not something I want to hear. How disgusting!*

"Um," I stammered, while trying to find something intelligent to say, utterly mortified.

"Yeah, I just can't seem to stop. In fact, I reckon I do it twelve, sometimes up to fifteen times a day!" he announced without so much as a flinch.

Why on earth is he telling me this? Isn't this a personal, private matter he should take to a professional? How does he expect me to respond?

I finally managed to clear my throat. "Look, Mick, I'm not the right person to be telling this sort of thing to." My hands shaking, I averted my eyes from him towards the menu board, pretending to study it, hoping I could change the subject to the healthy food selection.

"Oh, I thought you'd be the perfect person to help me. I'm obviously too horny to function properly, so I came to you for a suggestion," he smiled, leaning in, expectant of a response.

Heat penetrated every organ in my body, and the little spark in his eyes burned through me. I could feel my skin starting to sting. *Oh my God, this is this just an elaborate plan he's made up to get me to have sex with him! Is that how he wants me to help his "problem"?*

"Sorry, Mick, I can't help you," I answered, desperately wanting to run like hell, but I had already paid for my burger. I felt flustered, angry and pressured. I flat out changed the subject. He eventually took the hint.

It was the worst tofu burger I have ever eaten, but at least I learned something that day. Men must really think girls are stupid. Not only that, but where do they get it in their heads that they need to fool us into having sex with them? Are we not worthy of being asked out on a proper date? If he really did like me, as pointed out by my sister, then why not ask me out properly instead of all that rubbish? *Dickhead.*

His friend never asked me on a real date either. Back when I hung out with that group, of which Mick was part, this other guy, Glen, flat out propositioned me one night.

While we were sitting in his car waiting for our pizzas, he turned to me and said, "I have a little friend down there in need of some attention."

I ignored his lurid suggestion of performing oral sex on him, and a look of confusion came across his face.

"What's the matter? Dontcha give head?" he asked, perplexed.

I was gobsmacked. I was still only young and expecting boys to act like I thought they were supposed to, like young gentleman, asking girls on actual dates first.

Another male from that same group also had a similar approach. We were hanging out at the beach one night. There were six of us—three guys and three girls. We were all lying on the sand, gazing up at the sky, as most young people did on the coast in those days. The scene was ideal for romantic gestures. The other girls and I were half expecting the boys to put their arms around us, or chase us down to the water, maybe even try to steal a kiss. Any of that would have been fine.

"Wanna go up to the dunes and suck me off?"

I was completely shocked by the offer I got from that foul-mouthed grub, and my insides churned in repulsion.

I missed Mitchell, my first boyfriend, and wondered where he might be. I hoped he was happy. In that moment, I kicked myself, knowing I had probably made a huge mistake in letting go the one person who actually loved me and made me feel safe. I had so much more to learn at that age. I still do.

Chapter 22

Rushing out through customs at a New York airport, I searched the crowd for the man I had met online eight months earlier. I was lured with the prospect of finding a better man abroad, and it seemed to be the only travel opportunity I was going to get. I scrimped and saved and booked the cheapest flight I could find, because I needed this, desperately, if I was to try to stay out of the shadows of anxiety and depression.

I spotted him. He was smiling and waving, so I hurried over. We embraced, and it was pleasant. I liked his Puerto Rican looks. He had the shiniest, blackest hair I'd ever seen, and his accent sounded so exotic and romantic. Although I was exhausted, we chatted for the next four hours on the bus ride to Hartford, Connecticut, where he lived. I had already prepared myself for the chance it wouldn't work out, but at least I was going to have *one* big adventure.

What I wasn't ready for, was where I was going to be living exactly and what I was about to face. I thought I was finally getting away from the sexual harassment and everything else men continued to inflict upon me, but I didn't know that I was trying to escape the inescapable.

After settling myself in, I started to get the lay of the land. It disappointed me early on that my new man was gone at his job for so many hours every day and that I was left to fend for myself. Being trapped in a small studio apartment in what I was quickly discovering was an unfriendly neighbourhood wasn't how I pictured my exciting new adventure. I resolved that, because I had travelled so far and invested so much, I would just deal with whatever came my way graciously.

What was proving to be much more difficult to cope with, however, was the level of harassment I was receiving out on the streets. It was just as prolific as it was back home. The only difference was, the men who were following me, calling out to me and pulling up alongside me in their cars, were all drug-dealing criminal types, who I'm sure were all carrying weapons.

Our gun laws are very different in Australia. It is illegal to carry weapons of any kind, and for that reason alone, I felt somewhat safer in my own country.

It took every ounce of courage I could muster, borrowing a little from every person who had enriched my life with their gusto, just to walk to the end of the street to buy a carton of milk. Every time I stepped out, I was whistled at, leered at, followed and catcalled. The remarks they would make weren't quite as lewd as Aussie blokes.

"Hey baby doll, where you going?"

"Hey there girl, lookin' fine. Wanna come for a ride?"

"Damn Girl, you look good enough to eat!"

They weren't quite as vile or repulsive in comparison, but it was still harassment, and it bothered and worried me.

I was also facing a whole other raw and brutal world I was in no way prepared for. On this part of the planet, I had drug dealers offering me crack cocaine and weed, dark strangers approaching me for sex and money, homeless men harassing me for alcohol or cash and cars continuously pulling over next to me. They would cruise very slowly, in cars packed with suspicious-looking fellows who bopped their heads to thumping rap music, elbows jutting out, and leering at me while offering me rides and drugs.

Every day I had to pass by hooded men lurking in doorways, street gangs loitering about and sitting on hoods of cars, watching me as I walked by. Ragged people mumbled to themselves, sometimes yelling out profanities at any person they saw, including me. I passed men dressed as women, who stood waiting on street corners. And a guy with a face horribly disfigured by burn scars often tried to lure me into his apartment complex.

Cold shivers shot up my spine every time I heard the sound of sirens and what resembled gunfire. Every two hours or so, almost like clockwork, I felt a heavy pulse in my throat when I heard the voices calling up from outside my neighbour's window, "Yo fool, where da crack at?"

My boyfriend Juan failed to warn me that the apartment he picked out for us was in such a high-crime area and that I would be the only white-skinned person within a thirty kilometre radius, giving me another reason to stick out besides the fact that I was female. For such a hard-working, fairly educated guy, the area not only lowered him, but frightened the living hell out of me.

When I tried to give him a glimpse into what I had to endure every day by explaining about the harassment and the dangers I faced, he just shrugged indifferently. To him, his own neighbourhood was just something he drove in and out of completely unaffected by the cold savagery of the streets and therefore unable to grasp the fullness of what I was saying from a female's perspective.

I had just travelled all the way across to the other side the world for a man who threw me into a melting pot and abandoned me, leaving me to fend for myself with street smarts I didn't possess. I did my best with the little support he gave me, but I spent most of my time indoors, hiding away from my new world. It certainly wasn't the dream I had for myself, and I felt defeated and shrunken by it all.

When my visitor visa ran out, I had to return to Australia. In an odd sense, I felt more at ease with a world ruled by men who were more familiar to me. I could relax at the very least knowing that they weren't carrying guns.

Juan and I stayed in contact, and after six months, he jumped on a plane and joined me in Surfers Paradise. It was nice to spend that time with him again, but something between us had perished. Too much time had gone by, I suppose, and although I tried to make the most of his visit, I knew we were both more comfortable in our respective countries. He also had a young daughter who was dependent upon his weekend visits, and she needed him.

When it came time to say our final goodbyes, I took some comfort in the few friends I had and those that I had made online during my time away. One of the people I occasionally chatted to while Juan was away at work was an Australian bloke, James, who was living in Seattle at the time.

While spending my days alone and afraid in Hartford, James was one of many Aussies who hung out in an online chat group for ex pats. He popped up on my screen again after I returned to Australia. Months later, when I mentioned that my relationship was over and my man had returned to Connecticut, James almost immediately disappeared. It was really quite odd. He was never *not* online.

Five days later, he reappeared, but not online. He was now on the other end of my mobile phone. “It’s me, James from Seattle, well Queensland actually. I’m back in Australia!” he proudly announced, expecting me to be overjoyed.

What the hell?

“Oh hi,” I replied shocked and somewhat mortified, “how did you get my number?” I was more than curious.

“I did me some detective work!” he proclaimed. “But don’t worry ’bout that bit. How about we meet up?”

My skin crawled, and my mind raced, trying desperately to work out where he had surreptitiously extracted my number from. Then it twigged. Way back when we first started chatting, he hounded me about the exact location of a market stall I once tended on the weekends. It was very odd at the time why he wanted every tiny bit of information about it, but I didn’t think it mattered.

I quickly fit all the pieces together in my head. He must have flown back to Queensland immediately after I told him about my break up with Juan, then gone straight to the market office and asked for my number from management, who in an extreme breach of privacy gave it to him. I was livid. The audacity of this guy, and the market office!

His actions screamed, “desperate, sneaky, creepy guy who goes to colossal, privacy-breaching lengths for a minuscule chance of meeting a girl he barely knows." Who travels across the world for someone who just broke up with someone else? Warning, warning!

"Um, James, I'm kind of busy at the moment. I have to interview new flatmates, so I cannot meet you today. I'm sorry," I answered, furious that I had been put on the spot like this.

"Oh, come on. I just flew all the way . . . okay, how about tomorrow?" he sounded annoyed, yet hopeful.

"No, I can't. I'm busy," I answered, trying to nip him in the bud.

"So ya don't wanna see me, is that it?" he snipped.

How does he get to be upset with me? I don't owe this guy anything!

"James, you didn't tell me you were coming, and I have too much going on, sorry."

"Fine, s'pose I just wasted a shitload of time and money then!" he sulked then hung up.

I sighed heavily. *There goes another male with another bruised ego who wants to blame me for his misguided expectations.* At least my conscience was clear. I left the Internet alone for a while. From the many stories I was hearing about people encountering their own share of weirdo stalker types online, the novelty had definitely worn off.

Chapter 23

On the way home from shopping, I stopped at the traffic lights beside a car in the lane next to me. I never made a habit of looking over into another car, but for some reason, this time I did. I recognized the driver, a young man I had seen a few times around my apartment complex.

I was waiting for him to look over so I could give him a smile and wave. He did look over, but I didn't get anything like the reaction I was expecting. He gritted his teeth like a snarling beast, spat on the window then rammed his skull hard onto the glass, not once, but twice! He mouthed something ferocious at me that I could not hear, and from his angered face, it seemed he wanted to rip somebody's head off, namely mine! *Oh my!*

The second the light turned green, he sped off ahead of me. The two lanes merged, so I had no choice but to follow behind. I was completely terrified of this guy.

When I pulled up after him in our parking lot, he leapt from his car and banged on the hood of it, mouthing off at me again. He gave me a demonic, searing look, as if he was some devil robot trying to fry me with his laser beam eyes. I remained locked in my car until I watched him disappear into the apartments upstairs. He lived at the opposite end of the building to me, thank goodness. I assumed he was a heavy drug user. No bloke goes nuts like that without something seriously trippy in his system. Looking over at his car window, I noticed it was still smeared in salvia. My mind shot back to when I was nine years old.

I was walking along the path headed for the corner shop, when a boy I didn't recognize rode past on his bicycle. As he rode by me, he spat on my face. He got me good, right smack in the puss, sopping me with his gooey slime. A cold blanket of humiliation fell over me, and I felt about as low as a stain on a carpet.

Being so young, I wasn't sure if that happened to other

people or not and didn't know if it was considered normal behaviour. In my confusion and shame, I didn't tell anybody and have carried that around with me my entire life.

Driving to work the morning after my run in with Mr. Devil Robot, I approached a major roundabout that led early morning commuters onto the motorway. The traffic was already heavy, just like it was every morning, so I sleepily waited in the line-up, slowly inching my way towards the wagon wheel intersection.

An oversized transport truck that dwarfed me from behind insisted I pay it my full attention. It was much too close. I glanced into my rear-view mirror and could see a bearded man, mid-sixties, in a blue trucker singlet, giving me a spine-chilling wave with his fingers. His creepy finger tinkling was accompanied by a lecherous grin. I bolted upright.

He continued to inch up behind me. His wheels slowly rolled forward, closing the fraction of a gap we had between us. Millimetre by millimetre, he lurched forward. I crawled ahead as much as I could to allow more space between us without bumping into the car in front, but the trucker didn't want to allow any gap to come between us. He rolled forward again, and again I crept forward. This continued. He was now no more than a whisker from my bumper, towering behind me, casting a shadow of doom over my little car and tormenting me with his twisted game. I looked at my watch, it was only 7.32 a.m.

When it was finally my turn to go, I entered the roundabout. I drove around it until I reached my exit, then shot off onto the motorway. I cemented my foot to the accelerator and sped off ahead, hoping I could lose him.

It wasn't long before he caught up with me and began nipping at my heels once again. From my mirror, I could see him waving and smirking, letting me know he hadn't finished with me yet.

Two more trucks had now come tearing along, and they

took position, one on each side of me. They regulated their speed so we were all travelling at the maximum limit of 110 kilometres an hour. I wasn't entirely certain that they weren't all in communication with each other and had decided to band together for some early morning kicks. It could also have been a fluke. It didn't really matter. I was surrounded and frightened.

The lanes were packed, and the situation was becoming extremely dangerous. They weren't letting me out from their clutches, and we were travelling very fast. My peripheral vision was obscured by their trucks, which only allowed me to see the cars directly ahead. It was unnerving. I was trapped. This torment went on for about ten minutes, and I became so terrified that I was convinced a fatal accident was imminent.

The worst, most fearsome, perilous panic attack I have ever experienced came crashing over me. My head started to spin, and I felt I was tumbling in a barrel that had fallen over the edge of a waterfall. I frantically tried to stay focused on the road, but my head was swirling with such terror that my vision was almost completely blurred. I was dangerously close to losing control of my vehicle and crashing into the truck to my left. At any moment, I could potentially be smashed and battered and crushed into a mangled heap of twisted metal and explode into flames. This was it, I was about to die, and in the most horrific way.

Oh please, please, please, I don't want to go this way. I am so terrified. Please save me, please. My head is spinning so wildly, and I'm about to crash. Save me, somebody, please! Tears soaked my face. I felt my hand slipping on the wheel. This was it. I was starting to veer into the truck beside me.

It was as if my frantic plea was instantly answered, because at that very moment, an overwhelming sense of an almighty, powerful presence washed through me. It filled me with a peaceful reassurance. It was like heaven had released all of its angels forth just to save me. Whatever it was, I felt the force guide my hand and help me to straighten the wheel. I couldn't explain it, but I felt what seemed to be an invisible hand on top of mine. I blinked back the tears and refocused my eyes, the wheel now dead straight. I righted myself to a rigid attention.

I could see traffic congestion coming into view and cars ahead of me were starting to slow down. We all had to reduce our speed to a mere crawl. I never thought the sight of brake lights would mean so much to me. I went from sheer terror to ecstatic relief in the blink of an eye. Now if I did lose control of the steering wheel and veer into the truck next to me, our slow speed would render it nothing more than a bump. My life was going to be spared, and I received my miracle! *Thank you, thank you, thank you.*

The second I had the chance, I slipped into the outside lane and took the next exit. Just before I veered off, I eyed the two other truck drivers for the first time. They both smiled and tipped their caps to me. *Assholes.* Had I known I could have reported them for reckless endangerment, I would have done it, at least I think so. If that were to happen again today, I would report it without hesitation.

There was no way I was ever going to go back to the insanity of those motorways, and to this day I still never have. There is a trigger somewhere in my subconscious that fills me with panic if I even get near an onramp. Motorways, freeways, highways, or any roads that have a speed limit of 100 kilometres or more completely petrify me.

I have come to know the side roads very well, and they get me to where I need to go, safely and without fear of being messed with or killed. If I'm a little late, so be it. At least I'm alive.

* * *

I awoke to my new flatmate jiggling me. "Joy, wake up.

You’re screaming!” Kara said, standing over me, her eyes terrified.

It wasn’t the first time that I woke a flatmate, many having to shake me from my cries. Sometimes I remembered the nightmares, sometimes I wouldn’t. If I did recall them, they were always the same—being attacked, chased, threatened, raped, messed with or sexually assaulted in some way.

“Sorry, I didn’t mean to wake you,” I apologized.

“Oh no, don’t worry about me. You just sounded so tormented and distraught that I panicked and had to try and bring you out of it,” she said, placing her hand over her chest, trying to get her breath.

I had involuntarily frightened almost everyone I shared a flat with at some point, but couldn’t even begin to explain it and didn’t bother to try.

Chapter 24

Red flags frantically waved right in front on my face, yet I dismissed them all, allowing myself to fall for the ephemeral and hollow promises of a man with multiple addictions.

Brian lived upstairs. We were on nodding terms and occasionally shared a laugh and a chat, but when he first showed interest in me beyond being neighbourly, I should have run a hundred miles in the opposite direction.

Repeating the same stupid mistake I had made before with another, I believed his assurances that he was turning over a new leaf. I never questioned what was on the other side of that leaf or that he might not be sincere. I only saw the potential in him and took him on his word.

The only thing he was upfront about initially was the dire financial situation he had gotten himself into, which he "fixed" by rendering himself bankrupt. He filed the papers when we first started dating so that his debts were wiped clean before we went any further. That sounded fair to me, a decent thing to do surely. He was suspiciously tight-lipped about how he had gotten himself into so much debt in the first place, and because I didn't dig any deeper, I let my ignorance lead me into a relationship that was built upon deception and lies. I know now that it was the only way he could rope me in. The other evils that ruled his life only began revealing themselves once he knew I was committed.

I ignored the warnings, flicking away hints of concern that tapped upon my shoulders, foolishly overlooking his drinking and pot smoking habits, not yet comprehending the full extent of his dependency on both. His severe gambling addiction was what took the longest for me to discover—the reason for his bankruptcy and the most difficult one for him to admit. He kept the whole picture hidden from me for as long as he could, until I started noticing the signs.

Brian was a masterful liar, yet his charismatic charm and captivating smile weakened and fooled me. I overlooked everything in the early days, because I so desperately wanted to finally settle down and have some semblance of a stable and normal life.

Not long after we married, he admitted to serving time in prison. It was for various crimes, mostly robberies and drug dealings. I didn't know what I was more shocked about, the confessions or the crimes themselves.

For the next ten years, my stomach felt like a cement mixer filled with concrete bricks, constantly churning with thuds and clunks of anxiety and stress. While he spent his days and nights getting drunk and stoned, I sat at the kitchen table with the bills, exhausting myself while agonizing over our mounting debts. It was like trying to climb over a crumbling wall. Living with a fall-down, rotten drunk and habitual pot smoker with a serious gambling addiction was too much for me to handle. I tried, desperately, to keep our heads above water, but for every dollar I scrimped and saved to pay the bills, he frittered, smoked and drank away two.

Every night, I found him either passed out on the sofa or on the toilet floor. Within ten minutes of waking in the morning, he would pick up his putrid plastic juice bottle with a length of hose sticking out the end and have himself a hit. He seldom came home without stopping in at the pub first, most evenings arriving home late, wasted and broke.

I would often have to pick up pieces of smashed furniture and broken household items and cover my face in shame when he'd mouth off at almost every person he encountered. He constantly drove recklessly and dangerously while drunk and stoned, often instigating road-rage arguments, causing me a sickness in my stomach from embarrassment and humiliation.

There were many times I tried to walk away. He had become repugnant to me. I was completely done. When things would come to a head, and I told him I was leaving, he would apologize for his behaviour and promise he would quit his bad habits and turn over that new leaf. He kept me hanging in by a mere thread, crushing my spirit every time he broke his word. One minute he was apologizing, and the next, he was stealing my credit cards, money from my purse and items of mine that he would try to sell off for cash.

Whenever confronted about missing cash, his lies were the hardest to take. Without so much as a blink of an eye, he would claim the money simply fell out of his wallet and became lost. I foolishly believed him when he said he needed extra money for building supplies or work tools, until he repeatedly came home with neither. When I questioned him about it, he finally confessed that he was just keeping the money for himself, gambling it and paying off his drug debts.

Mounting credit card debt didn't help. Brian had somehow amassed that to around $11,000, adding to the mortgage debt that was solely in my name. He would badger me to use the equity of the house, which there was barely any of, to finance a new ute for him. Additionally, he would push me to use my good credit standing to get him a credit card of his own, because his bankruptcy had left him blacklisted. Completely devious and opportunistic, he used me to benefit himself in any way he could.

I barely ever slept a wink. Our marriage was misery, occasionally interrupted by a friendly hug. I needed someone to slap me in the face and shake sense into me. He wasn't ever going to change. When he finally admitted that he didn't want to give up any of his habits, not even to save our marriage, it left me very little choice.

That is what addiction does. It robs you of everything that is important in your life. Your relationships, home, family, finances, job, credibility, respect, health, wellbeing and your peace of mind, all forfeited for the selfish need of some fleeting high.

Ten years of my life were wasted on that man. An entire decade of my love, trust, patience and understanding were spent waiting and hoping for the day he would fulfill his promise to me. Every waking moment I felt sick, anxious, sad, disappointed and angry. It was no marriage. It was a prison sentence I was serving without having committed a crime.

From start to finish, Brian had gambled away over $80,000. I almost fell off my chair when I did the math, and the truth was revealed in black and white. That was money we could have put towards the mortgage, car insurance, much needed renovations, repairs and other vital necessities.

As I headed out the door for the final time, Brian said, "You were the best thing that eva happened to me."

I appreciated his words, but I knew if I stood there a moment longer, he would more than likely start blaming me for something he resented me for. Most of our marriage he made damn sure I knew he begrudged me for being someone he wasn't—a responsible, level-headed, dependency-free person.

* * *

I walked out of the marriage and into an extended round of sexual harassment once again. I had continued to be harassed throughout the duration of our marriage as well, but it didn't seem to matter to Brian.

If I was waiting for him to come out from the pub, I would often hear the offers.

"If your man aint payin' you attention, Luv, then we can show ya a good time!"

"Why dontcha leave that loser ya waitin' for and come drink with some real men?"

"If he ain't comin' out sweedart, you can take me 'ome!"

There were times I would be standing right beside Brian and they would say to him, "Struth mate, you got lucky! You wanna share?" Brian usually just laughed. I tried to be good-natured about the comments and somehow mustered a tight-lipped smile, but it always bothered me that my husband didn't care.

After I left him, I removed my wedding ring and moved out on my own, into a basement apartment below a young couple with twin baby girls. I continued on with my life as usual and plodded back and forth to work, cooked my meals, slept, cleaned and did my grocery shopping, trying to piece together the fragments of my shattered spirit.

It was a sad and difficult time, but simultaneously, I was happy to be away from him and his drug habit. It made me so happy that I could finally sit on the sofa any time without Brian's passed-out-drunk lump taking up the whole thing. There was no need to hide my purse or my credit cards anymore, and it was wonderful to no longer find stinky bong spillages everywhere. I also rather enjoyed having the entire fridge to myself, and so I filled it with fresh fruits and vegetables instead of beer.

What I had wasn't much, but I had it all to myself and no longer feared anything being destroyed or stolen. Finally, I felt peaceful instead of being startled awake by the smashing of beer bottles into the recycling bin, crushing any memory of my dreams.

* * *

On one of my regular grocery-shopping days, I headed towards the fruit and vegetable barn as I always did, and a casually dressed man, I guessed in his sixties, was standing outside speaking into a microphone. I hadn't seen this man before, and I'd shopped there for years. He was letting customers know about their specials for the week.

I walked past him and smiled like I would at anybody, forgetting that I had to be careful about doing that. I grabbed a shopping cart and headed down to the far aisle to pick out a few potatoes. It suddenly became quiet, as the man on the microphone stopped talking. I looked up and noticed that he was walking towards me, sauntering all the way to the back of the store, bypassing two other staff members.

"Can I help you?" he asked. There was something about him that irked me. Maybe it was his approach or something peculiar in his eyes, but my gut told me he wasn't being genuine. The fact that he was staring at my chest and not at my face gave me enough reason to put up my safety shield.

"No thanks," I smiled, returning to the mound of golden tubers.

My abrupt answer caused his eyes to dart frantically about searching for a new direction. "So what are you planning on doing with those?" he plucked from the air.

"Cook them!" I smiled again, giving him nothing more of me. It was not my intention to be rude. I have been more than polite to so many who didn't deserve it, but I just didn't like the look of this guy. It was something I'm sure my history had a lot to do with. I did feel a little bad for him though. It wasn't his fault that so much had tainted me to such an acute level of apprehension and suspicion.

Leaving him with nothing further to work with, he left me and meandered back to the front of the store where he picked up his microphone and continued on with his spiel.

When I had filled my cart with more than enough healthy food for the next month, I paid at the register and walked past him again. I pushed my cart out into the parking area and wheeled it over to the farthest row in the lot, where my car was sitting. The very end row was the only place I could find any shade from the few trees that bordered the shopping complex, and in our searing summer temperatures, I needed every bit of what those trees offered.

After unlocking my car, I turned to start unloading my groceries from the cart, but someone had already started grabbing my bags. It startled me. I looked up to see who the hell was touching my stuff. It was that guy. Mr. Potato Head, minus one microphone.

"Here, I'll give you a hand," he announced, frightening me mightily. He had obviously followed me. I immediately remembered that sick, twisted stalker who followed me home after work in his car all those years ago. I felt completely rattled. *Man I hate being followed! What am I supposed to do, be grateful for the help? Or should I have every right to feel tense because he silently trailed after me, uninvited, all the way to the quietest and farthest part of the complex?* Maybe I was being paranoid, maybe I wasn't, but because I didn't want to appear rude or impolite, I let him finish helping me and then thanked him for his assistance.

"S'orright!" he said. "Maybe I'll see you again sometime?"

"Oh, maybe," I replied. *Oh no, please, I don't want to start a whole thing.*

"If you ever wanna go for coffee, you let me know," he offered.

I looked at his face, and he shot me a wink and a smirk that I knew very well. My entire body filled with hot prickles.

"Oh, um, well, I'm very busy." I opened my car door and got in. "Okay, bye!" I slipped the key into the ignition and turned it. I reversed out of the car space and pulled away without another word.

As I drove away, I thought how difficult it must be for men. This guy didn't really do anything that bad, but if he didn't have that stalker element attached to his approach, maybe I would have chatted to him and the offer for an actual coffee date might have been more tempting.

On another day in the same shopping complex, I was followed by another man in almost exactly the same way. I was in the post office being served by my usual sales clerk who knew me as a regular customer. A man standing behind me—he looked late fifties, wearing trucker shorts and flip flops—must have overheard my conversation with her about not needing a Valentine's Day card that year.

I didn't think. I had just let this bloke know that I was single and alone. *Stupid, stupid.* He then decided to follow me to my car. I was parked in that same far row where I usually parked under the shade. Unbeknownst to me, he was walking behind me the entire way.

Once at my vehicle, he made the same sudden appearance from behind as Mr. Potato Head had. "'Scuse me, Miss. I overheard ya back there sayin' ya don't need a Valentine card this year, so I thought if I gave you my number, you could call me and . . ."

"No thanks!" I interrupted, putting my hand up.

"Geez, lady, I was only just askin'," he snipped and huffed off.

A blue sedan then pulled up beside me and a younger man leaned out of his window.

"Are you okay, Miss? I saw that guy following you, so I followed him following you," he explained.

Oh this is getting to be quite a day!

"Oh, I'm okay, thanks," I replied. "Thanks for looking out for me though." I smiled. I slipped into my car and sped off home feeling rather spooked. It was at least nice to know somebody was looking out for me if nothing else. That was rare.

The following week, I had to deal with a bunch of guys catcalling me from the outdoor patio of the pub directly across the road from the same shopping complex. They hooted and whistled and called out something I couldn't quite understand, but I did hear the word *baby.* I guess that's all I'd ever be to them, even in my mid-forties.

Chapter 25

For absolutely no reason that I could comprehend, I started receiving X-rated text messages on my mobile phone. They were being sent from a number I did not recognize. I considered it could have been Brian, but dismissed it after remembering how lazy he was. He simply wouldn't have been bothered. He did many things, but sending filthy messages to his ex-wife was just not something he would spend his time, money or energy on.

From the explicit content, I could tell it was a male on the other end. Every few minutes, I received another message. They were so vile they made me feel sick.

"I wanna fuck u hard & cum all over yr face"

"Im gunna ram u so hard, u will scream 4 mercy"

"Do u like it rough? I betcha do"

I kept my phone in my purse while I was working, but I could hear it chiming away. When I had a moment's break, I'd scroll through them.

"I have a big hard cock 4 u"

"Do u swallow?"

"Pinch your nipples & rub your clit 4 me"

And more.

This continued for hours. I was beginning to feel beaten down by this guy, finding it increasingly more difficult to concentrate on my job. I was surprised at how much he could think up! The messages were extremely hard to ignore, being so vulgar and violating, which led me to the point where I was at a loss as to what to do. *How do I stop this?* I thought if I didn't respond at all, which I didn't, maybe he would simply just run out of steam.

Not only didn't he run out of steam, but continued with his torment all morning, all through lunch and well into the afternoon. By dinnertime, I was distraught. This freak hadn't let up at all, and he had completely trashed my entire day.

I had to do something. I decided to send my first reply:

"You are a pest. Stop now, or I'll call the police!" It not only didn't stop him, but my reply also just seemed to fuel his fire.

"Ooh u r a feisty one. I like a kitty that scratches! Cum on, spit on me, pleeze!" he sent, and continued sending more and more like these well into the evening.

I spent the remainder of my night desperately trying to find a way to block the messages from coming in. I messaged everybody I knew, but nobody could help. I then felt no choice but to call the police.

I was stunned when I was told they couldn't do anything unless I was receiving actual threats to my life. So I called the phone company. They suggested I try putting that number into a group and then block that entire group, but only certain phones had the ability to do that, and mine didn't. Why isn't there a function on *all* phones that can protect people from this type of thing?

There was no question that I was being harassed, sexually harassed, and yet I was being told that nobody could do anything. Not one person could help me, and I felt so lost. I considered many times calling the number, but then what? Do I make some kind of threat? I've never made a threat in my life, and I was much too frightened of what was on the other side of that phone and what dangers I might potentially face. By the time I climbed into my bed that evening, I had counted 168 texts, each one filthy and sickening. I deleted them all. They violated me.

Even under the soft shelter of my blanket, my skin crawled, my head pounded and my stomach hurt. I managed only a few tortured hours of broken sleep.

At around half past six, I awoke to the chiming of my phone. New messages began arriving one after the other with delirious force.

"Morning sunshine, did u think u were safe? think again!"

"U r not rid of me yet!"

"Do u like a stiff cock b4 breakfast?"

"Turn over so I can ram my rod up u?"

"Want it up the ass petal?"

I sat on the edge of my bed, slumped with my head in my hands, exhausted already.

From within the central command of my gut, I could hear my own voice. It was giving me advice. *Don't let this low-life scumbag get to me. Be strong, get up, get dressed and face the day.* I couldn't afford to take the day off, so I listened to myself and did what I said.

It was at the many moments like these when I knew, without question, there was a presence in my life, always helping and guiding me. The voice sounded like me, but the words came from a higher power, which communicated with me in a voice I wouldn't so easily dismiss. I felt blessed that I understood that.

The messages continued all that day and long into that night. I couldn't help but think that surely he would run out of things to say. *Who is this freak?* I didn't think it was anyone I knew, so I couldn't understand why I was being targeted. My number could have belonged to anyone, and yet he was relentlessly sending these abhorrent texts to a seemingly random stranger. I could have been a cop for all he knew. *Or* did *he know me?*

Panic started to rise up. *What if he does know who I am, where I live and where I am right now? What if he has been following me? What if he is sitting outside in his car watching me?* Men had done it before. I was too frightened to check out my window to see. I scurried about my flat, double checking all the locks and reassuring myself everything was closed good and tight. I then climbed into bed.

By the end of that evening, he had sent another 87 messages. What a colossal waste of energy, time and money, and all for what purpose? I never even replied, except for that once, so without any response, I would have assumed he would have lost all interest by now.

It was around midnight when I received the last message

for the day.

"Nite precious, I'll be dreaming of u all tied up, begging me to rape u!"

Another night of my much-needed sleep was lost to the evils of another disturbed individual.

At the very break of dawn, my phone chimed again. It was the first message of another round of torturous texts.

"Did u dream of eating cock last nite sweetheart?"

I couldn't even stomach breakfast. I wished that I didn't even need my damn phone, and that I could just toss it into the ocean, or at least get a new number, but it was indispensable—particularly for keeping in touch with my clients. For the last couple of years, I had been making an honest day's living from cleaning homes, not exactly what I had envisioned for myself, but it paid the bills. The world was supposed to be full of exciting possibilities, but it actually narrowed down to only a few, and here I was, scrubbing toilets.

I can't let this sicko ruin my livelihood. Why should I have to go to all the expense and hassle of changing my number, while this creep gets away with his sick game, getting his cheap thrills? No, I'm not going to do that. I don't want to be the same pushover I once was. I was trying not be anyway. Baby steps.

My landlords upstairs, the lovely young couple with twin baby girls, were home when I knocked on their door. I wanted to pay my rent before leaving for work and they invited me in. My phone chimed three times in the six minutes I was there, and they noticed my distress. The husband asked what the matter was, so I handed him my phone with an explanation.

"I don't know who this person is, and it's been three days like this," I told them.

He looked at me, furrowed his brow, and while still holding my phone, started pressing numbers on my keypad. He then lifted the phone to his ear, waiting. His wife and I looked at each other and shrugged our shoulders, left only to guess what he was doing, assuming he was dialling the number.

"Voicemail," the husband mouthed, waiting for the end of his message. "Yeah, listen here mate. I don't know who the hell you think you are, but you keep texting my wife and I'm gunna find out where ya live and come over there and bash your fuckin' head in!"

Oh my goodness!

"There, that should get rid of him for ya!" he smiled, handing me back my phone.

Wow!

The messages stopped immediately. I was stunned, mortified and overjoyed simultaneously. I couldn't believe it was so simple! What a genius, and all it took was for a male to intervene. It is amazing how that works. Men won't listen to us when *we* tell them to stop, but when another male does, then it's, "Yes, sir!"

Peace was restored once again to its rightful place within my household of one, and my appetite returned along with it, not only for food, but for life.

* * *

I stumbled across an ad for a social group. Perhaps the universe knew I was ready to start living again. It read: "Social activities and fun-filled events". That sounded like exactly what I needed. I signed up then and there.

Two weeks later, I got myself ready and walked into an already bustling restaurant without knowing a single soul. Drawing in a deep breath, trying to pluck some courage from the air, I smiled and introduced myself around. Within a few hours, I had been *friended* on people's social media accounts, which was this new way of connecting that I had to get myself acquainted with.

The world seemed to have become a very frantic place,

with networking individuals palming electronic devices and speaking about *tweeting* this and *instagramming* that. I felt old.

The worst part of my new social life was when people would flash their phones in front of my eyes to show me something, and I had to say, "Sorry wait, I can't see without my glasses. They are in my purse somewhere. Hold on." They would just roll their eyes impatiently and move on to other things.

Despite this new contemporary world, most of the members seemed friendly and always up for some fun, exactly the kind of people I needed to be around. I wanted to let my hair down and live a little. I had been caged in marriage hell with an addict for the last ten years and needed to find myself again and rediscover who I was. If I could do that through picnics, dinners out, games nights and dancing, then I wanted to jump in with both feet.

I made fast friends with lots of girls, but I felt reserved amongst the males in the group. One guy I just met, Asian appearance, nice looking with an Australian accent who I immediately found intriguing, asked for my number. Before I could even speak, he snatched my phone from my hand. I didn't know what was happening. I quickly learned that apparently people add themselves to each other's contact lists now, instead of using the traditional pen and paper I once knew.

On my screen, I had a photo of me at my mother's eightieth birthday party. I was wearing a nice dress and didn't mind how I looked for once. The guy who had taken my phone saw it and decided to play a little game. He touched his finger to my screen and simulated tickling my crotch on the photo. "Mmm, can you feel that?" he snickered.

I took my phone back, disappointed because when I first met him, I wanted to give this guy my full respect, but after that I didn't see why I should.

A few other guys in the group put the moves on me almost

immediately, but they soon found out I didn't join just to be their sexual conquest.

After one particular night out dancing, the party continued on at the home of one of the members. Nothing had changed much in the way of partying since my day. Everybody still got good and drunk, some smoked pot, some popped little pills and the subject inevitably would turn into something sexual, so nothing new or surprising there.

Being that I still wasn't a drinker, I always had my wits about me, so when one of the guys shoved his hand down into my pants when we were left alone together in an upstairs room, I quickly grabbed it to stop him from clawing at my crotch. It took every ounce of fight I had to fend him off, as he had the strength of a Marine. With echoes of the past lurching forward to help me in the struggle, I finally got him to release me. He eventually passed out drunk right next to me.

I slipped away, almost leaving the group then and there, but was told to just brush it off. He apparently was that way with every new female. Not at all comforting or helpful, but I stayed anyway, albeit on high alert.

Again, not even a week later, another male member tried slipping his hands under my top while cornering me in the bathroom. He came in and tried to plant his beer-soaked lips on me while his hands grabbed at all my lady parts. My veins filled with old panic, and I shoved him away, managing to slink out from under his armpit.

When I talked about it with the other girls, they just laughed. Most of the girls in the group had unwittingly been cajoled into having sex with these guys already. They had all been given false promises of forming potential relationships, only to realize later they had all been duped. When I asked them how they all managed to stay friends with them afterwards, they just shrugged it off. It was as if being used and abused didn't bother them, but I saw something else in their eyes.

On another night out, I was followed around the entire evening by someone new to our club. He clung to me like a bur from a prickle bush with the assumption that I was now his property. The more he drank, the closer he got. I did everything to give him the message that I wasn't interested—looking away, talking to my friends, dancing in a group, avoiding eye contact—but he didn't take the hint. He tried to lay claims on me, putting his arm around me, calling me "Babe" and whispering in my ear. I couldn't go five minutes without him looking for me or asking where I was.

His persistence in hanging around was not a positive quality, not at all charming, and he was ruining my night. I felt suffocated and couldn't take another minute of it. He left me no choice but to leave. I waited for the opportune moment and gave him the slip while he went to the bathroom.

I dashed off to my car, praying he wouldn't find me and follow me home. It was a familiar ending to many nights out I'd had in the past: being pestered, harassed, frightened and having to escape the clutches of another persistent male.

This was another reason why I stuck it out for so long in my marriage. As soul destroying as it was, I often weighed up my options, thinking it preferable to stick with it, rather than jump back into the ocean amongst the sharks. I was damned if I stayed and damned if I didn't. Nevertheless, I was back out there, and once again having to be on guard every moment.

There are no easy choices when you are trying to survive being a single woman. It is like trying to navigate through a minefield, one wrong move and it could be your last.

I didn't have to go out. I realized this of course. But where was it written that the act of going out and trying to enjoy myself (like the rest of the world) automatically sanctioned men to hound and pester me into being a bed partner? Was I not entitled to what guys take for granted? To be able to go out and have fun without fear? It wasn't like we were going to the nightclubs of Surfers Paradise or to sleazy pick-up bars. We chose venues that catered to our age group, places with some element of class and style, with a more civilized atmosphere, where we thought adults knew how to behave. These places were now popping up everywhere. The coast had not only grown, it had exploded into a thriving, bustling metropolis over the last fifteen years.

The following month, a number of us from our group decided to go along to the AC/DC concert. Not all of us could afford tickets, but we went anyway just for something to do. It was a fair walk to the venue, but we didn't mind. The atmosphere was electric, as thousands of loyal fans made their way to the stadium, singing, calling out, cheering and whistling. We overheard two young males walking ahead of us, saying they had a spare ticket. Without thinking, I sung out, "I need a ticket. How much?"

The guy on the left turned half way around, grabbed his crotch and said, "Two hundred bucks, and you can give me a blow job too!"

I was so stunned I couldn't even find words to reply. I just could never get used to males responding so inappropriately and disrespectfully. It was as if it were an Australian law that males had to be as crude as they possibly could.

"Forget it," I said, letting them walk off ahead.

The next weekend, a few of us were having a couple of drinks at a quiet bar. I was sipping on a Coke and having a nice time, enjoying the ambient music and having a chat with my friends. For some reason, I felt I was being watched. I looked over and eyed a weathered-looking man, I guessed in his sixties, staring at me. He was unquestionably leering, motionless and fixated.

Nothing that was going on around him seemed to break his luridly long gaze. I tried returning to my conversation with my friends, but they were equally bothered by him. He continued to stare for at least ten minutes, which was nine minutes and fifty seconds too long. Every time I glanced to see if he was still staring, he was, as if hell-bent on tormenting me.

One of the male members of the group saw what was going on and decided to take this guy on. He began to stare back. Soon, the rest of us were spectators to a fierce battle of the eyeballs. Brows became furrowed, eyes became slits and mouths turned into snarls. After about one full minute, the old geezer finally broke. He rose from his chair and left, petulant.

I was getting too old for this crap.

Chapter 26

I had been cleaning homes for a while and had a range of clients from career-minded singles and hard-working families to wealthy property developers. I needed the work desperately because Brian had sent me documents.

If he hadn't done enough to me already, my soul destroying ex wasn't happy unless he stripped me of every lousy thing I had left to survive on. Being the letch that he was, it was clear his intention was to hurt me as much as humanly possible. I needed every dollar to fight him in court. I couldn't miss a day of work.

When I turned up at my Wednesday client's home, I was surprised to be met by a plumber who was there doing repairs. He was mid-fifties, at a guess, already dirty and sweating. He introduced himself and explained that we had to try to work around each other. That was fine. I could be accommodating.

Around 12.15 p.m., the tool-belted tradesman stopped to have his lunch. He plopped himself down on a stool at the kitchen counter, the very one I had just cleaned, and started tucking in to the contents of his lunch box. I decided to pour myself a glass of water at that time, which invited us to have some light conversation. From where I was standing, I could clearly see his pair of lily-white bum cheeks that were jutting out from his shorts. They were divided by a dark, furry crack. If he had worn a shirt that actually fit him, I would have been saved the unsightly display of his oversized behind. I pretended not to notice. He then asked me what I was doing on the weekend.

"I'm actually going on a farm stay with a social group I belong to," I answered. I was really quite excited about going, because it was my first time doing anything fun like this with a group of people. I hadn't been on a farm since I was a young child and was hoping to get up close to some cows. I didn't tell him that, however, I would have sounded like a dork.

"So this 'social' group ya say you're in," he *quoted* with two fingers in the air, "are youse all gunna be sleeping together orgy style at this farm or what?" he asked, raising his eyebrows. Rolls of skin appeared on his forehead.

Wow, this is what he took from "social group"?

"Goodness no!" I answered immediately, "Some might sleep with each other, but it's not *that* sort of group!"

"Why not?" he asked. "Sounds like you'd enjoy a bit of *that* kind of fun!" he smirked.

What the hell was that supposed to mean? How could he possibly make that kind of judgment upon me so quickly? The nerve of this jerk! I wanted to throw my glass of water right in his face.

"I better get back to work," I said, not even bothering to respond. I returned to the vacuum cleaner a few feet away and brutally yanked on the cord from the back. If he hadn't guessed already, I was now ticked off. I turned the machine on and drowned him out.

When I finished cleaning the carpets about half an hour later, I entered the laundry to prepare my mop and bucket. I lowered the bucket into the sink, turned on the hot water and watched it while it filled. Mr. Butt Crack appeared in the doorway.

"So have ya gotnee juicy stories about this 'social' club you're in?" He did the air quotes again.

What the hell?

"No," I answered, keeping my eyes on my filling bucket.

"Oh c'mon. Surely ya got something naughty you can tell me!" he pestered. "So you'se all doin' each other or what? It's a fuck club isn't it, really?"

How am I supposed to respond to that? Where does this guy get off? I wanted to really give it to him. I had all the words ready to deliver, but I needed my old friend Chloe to say them for me. I wasn't quite courageous enough. I also worried that I could be either insulted further or goodness knows what. Being alone in a house with someone who had sex on their brains was enough to make me worry about what could potentially happen. I had to find a way to answer without being rude and without leading him on at the same time. Trying to be friendly and polite to someone while being harassed and annoyed by them was horrible. I had been forced into this awkward position time and time again, and it was exhausting, stressful and irritating.

"As if!" I said, annoyed that it was the best response I could come up with.

"Aah, I reckon ya got some dirty stories you could tell me," he pressed. "I'd love to hear some of 'em!"

"It's a social club. We just go out to dinner, have games nights and attend events and outings. If anybody is having sex, then that's not anyone's business." I couldn't believe I had to explain this to a stranger.

"So you're telling me thatcha got no naughty stuff to tell me?"

"No!" I snipped. I didn't want to answer his questions anymore and just wanted to be left alone and get back to my job.

When the soap bubbles reached the top of my bucket, I lifted it from the tub and carried it out. I then headed to the far end of the house, well away from Mr. Butt Crack.

A few minutes later, I heard the front door open. It was the owner returning home early. I exhaled in relief, knowing I was finally rescued. I never told my client about the harassment. I was unaware that his actions were actually more serious than I understood, but thankfully it was the last I saw of him.

I had a similar experience in the home of another client a few weeks later. That time, he was a lot more dangerous looking and not someone I wanted messing with me.

When I turned up to my Friday client's home, I was met by a very large man wearing a black Harley-Davidson T-shirt. He had dragons and snakes tattooed all over his arms and hands. His fingers were adorned with chunky silver rings. One I noticed was shaped like a skull. I guessed his age to be late fifties. He looked very similar to someone who showed up looking to rent my room years ago. I recalled the moment when I showed him the bathroom. After seeing the shower, he had winked and said, "Ooh room for two!" That was when I decided to choose Chloe to move in.

The man I was now confronted with at my client's house did have an appearance that was quite intimidating, but I didn't want to start my day off feeling frightened or judgemental. I decided to give him the benefit of the doubt that he was perfectly harmless.

"Hi, I'm the cleaner," I smiled.

"Yeah, I know," he replied. "I've been expecting ya!" He then went on to explain that he was a friend of the owners, who without letting me know, had gone away for two weeks. He was there to housesit, and apparently my cleaning services were part of the deal.

"Okay, well nice to meet you. I'll get on with it then," I said and headed off into the master bathroom. I always started there.

About half an hour later, while scrubbing the shower, I was startled by his sudden appearance. That was the second time this guy had surprised and alarmed me that day.

"Sorry luv, didn't mean to rattle ya, but I just wanted to say that if ya get too hot from all that scrubbin', then you could come out and 'ave a cool down in the swimmin' pool," he offered.

Sure, it wasn't his place, so why not take advantage of all its luxuries.

"Oh, thanks, but I better keep going. I have a lot to do and only so much time to get it all done," I replied.

"Yeah sweet as, just thought I'd offer. I'll be goin' in shortly myself if you change your mind but!" he added.

"Oh thanks, but I don't even have my swimming costume. Besides, after I'm finished here, I have another house to do so . . ."

"Well you don't 'avta worry 'bout that. You can just strip everything off if ya want. I'll even join ya!"

Okay, I am fairly sure that I am being hit on.

"Thanks, but I have to get back to work now," I deflected, hoping he would leave.

"Righto then, well if ya get too hot or had enough of work and wanna 'ave a bit of fun, ya know where to find me dontcha?"

"Yep!" I smiled, retreating.

The next few hours couldn't go quickly enough. All I did was worry about being alone in a house with some huge beast of a guy who was eager to get me naked in the pool.

He appeared twice more, causing me near heart failure each time.

"Just checkin' up on ya!" he claimed.

"Oh, thanks, but I'm okay," I responded. Finally, by three o'clock, I was finished.

"Well that's me done for day. I'll get out of your way now." I said on my way out.

"Ya goin' already?"

"Yes, I have to go and clean another house now. It was nice to meet you. See you next time!" I said as politely as I could.

"So when ya finish your other job, why dontcha come back so we can have that swim together," he winked.

I was so sick and tired of this shit.

"No, I can't, sorry. I have to rush home and then go out to meet my friends," I lied. *Why do I have to justify myself for not wanting to get naked with a stranger?*

"Okay, well I'll be here all week if you ever want that swim!" he called out as I closed the door.

They don't get it, do they? Badgering a woman is not going to work—it is harassment.

At the end of that month, the husband of another regular client came home while I was cleaning the kitchen. After we exchanged some pleasantries, he came out and told me, "A mate of mine gets his house cleaned by a girl who goes topless!"

Okay, so?

"Yeah, he pays her extra though!"

Okay, I think I see where this is going.

"Yeah my wife doesn't let me see her naked anymore," he started grumbling. "So how are you off financially?"

He couldn't be less subtle. I wasn't about to give anyone "pity titties." I had no idea how to respond. I had spent a lifetime doing everything possible to keep my naked body protected from men, who had done everything in their power to try to violate it, so no amount of money would ever entice me to willingly show any part of it off to them. They had already taken enough from me, so I wasn't about to give up what little I had left. *No, absolutely not, never ever.*

I might have been a tad rude, but I gave him the brush off by continuing to busy myself. I was hoping he would take my silence as an answer. Thankfully, he did.

For as long as I could remember, despite my concerted efforts to feel like somebody, anybody in this world, I had constantly been reminded that I was nothing more than a cheap piece of ass. As I drove home that day, new tears started to pool in my eyes. I was *definitely* too old to still be feeling this way.

Chapter 27

I couldn't bring myself to read one more message, yet I still had 280 more waiting for me in my inbox. This online dating thing was going to be a colossal waste of my time—the very reason I resisted filling out my profile in the first place.

The few that I *did* open were not inspiring.

"Geez u look good. Wanna meet?"

"I like what I see. How about a date tonite?"

"Hey baby what u doing. Want me to cum over?"

"Are you into snakes?"

"I got a fuck load of shit on YouTube. Check me out"

"Got any naked pics?"

Message after message, I received barely anything more than cheap propositions for sex, and even those who did go to the trouble of actually constructing an entire paragraph, still made no effort to spell correctly or even punctuate.

After twelve months of having been separated from Brian, I felt ready to start looking for another man again. I had done what I had set out to do and reconnected with the part of me that needed a boost after my disastrous marriage. I had had some fun and lived a little, but I still couldn't deny my ultimate quest for real love. Somewhere deep within my marrow, I knew the love of my life was still out there.

I imagined him. He would be doing something meaningful with his life, whatever it may be. Not only would he be a true gentleman in every sense of the word, but he would also be searching for someone like me to be by his side. We could discover nature's most exquisite planet together. We could travel, write, explore and feel connected to each other by something we drew vital breath from. I didn't hold out much hope in finding him on the Internet, but there was an intense voice inside me telling me otherwise. It was as if I were being told to wait patiently, sit tight, and he would find me. So against my better judgement, that is exactly what I did.

The single men who had presented themselves in the first

week of signing up were an expected disappointment, but I resolved that I was doing what the universe was telling me to do. At least I was safe from the dangers of going out and from all that drunken, feral behaviour associated with it. If I waited online, I could avoid being potentially groped, pestered, followed, stalked, stared at, abused, harassed, physically assaulted or raped. I had had my fill of that already.

Closing the lid of my laptop, I settled on the sofa where I soon drifted into a blank trance. A surge of searing cramps came from within my uterus, as if a bomb had detonated inside me. I knew instantly it was the onset of my monthly lady time. Dashing into the bathroom, I opened the cupboard underneath the sink and took out a sanitary napkin from the packet. I did my woman things, and then I swallowed a couple of Aspirin down with a glass of water. Shuffling hunched over into the kitchen, I looked up at the calendar. *Right on time.*

A few minutes later, I was lying back on the sofa and realized I had forgotten to fill my hot water bottle. The heat always helped, along with painkillers, to ease me through my extremely painful, heavy periods. I tried willing myself to get up again to fetch it, but I struggled against the sharp jabs in my abdomen. I was actually glad to be alone in that moment, preferring the solitude during my "special" time every month.

There was not one thing that was special about it. I suffered tremendously. Not only did I feel painful cramps in my belly, but also my lower back ached, as did my legs all the way down to my feet, particularly the insides of my thighs. My whole body felt weak. My breasts would become extremely tender. I felt sick. Food smells made me ill. Noise and light gave me headaches, and I felt so emotionally raw that I struggled to cope with even the smallest things. It had been the same way every month since I turned thirteen.

Suffering through these every month when I was in a

relationship was made that much worse because the men in my life never understood what I went through. They weren't exactly supportive or helpful to me.

"Oh it's moody bitch time again, is it? I better duck for cover!"

"Oh, here we go. Watcha gunna cry about this time?"

"Eww, stay away from me when you got those things!"

"How long is this one gunna last? A man has needs you know!"

If I became tearful because of their insensitivity, they would blame me and my "time" instead of their hurtful words or attitudes.

When I was eighteen, I was returning from the supermarket with my feminine products in a thin plastic grocery bag. I was in the middle of a very heavy cycle and feeling like I was having the very life drained out of me. A car full of young blokes driving by saw what I was carrying. One of them called out, "On ya rags are ya?!"

I shrank with embarrassment.

The three of them then joined in a chorus of, "Lookie, lookie, she's got her rags. Haha, she's got her rags!" They taunted, hooted and hollered, mocking me while they drove by.

Tears suddenly flooded my eyes, and I dashed home, feeling as though I were back in the toilet block at school, being teased and tormented by the older, and much nastier, girls for the very same thing. What was supposed to be a very natural, normal part of any young woman's life had become a shameful and demeaning experience, which started as soon as I hit puberty. I have carried the echoes of those days around with me each month, every month for as long as I can remember.

* * *

After sifting through my growing list of messages over the

following week, I forced myself to accept a date with someone who seemed to be not quite as bad as the others. I went out with him to prove I could be courageous enough to do it. I wanted to be strong and try to conquer my debilitating nerves about meeting men I didn't know. I was nowhere near as resilient or as brave as I had hoped. It took me almost thirty trips to the loo before I could even walk out the door. Whenever anxiety built up in my body, my nerves would trigger my bladder, causing me to make more visits to the bathroom than anyone I had ever known.

A few hours after walking out the door, I ran back in, traumatized from my date. I was not only propositioned for sex, I was slobbered all over and claimed as my date's new girlfriend immediately. Even worse, I was told I was going to be a new stepmother to a twelve year old boy! I was about to delete my profile right then and there, but I went to bed instead. It was lucky that I did.

The following morning, I felt a strong urge to open just one last little envelope. I really didn't think I could stomach facing another whack job, so I braced myself for the worst. I clicked it open. *What's this?*

The person who had written *this* message had not only written more than one line, he had written more than one sentence! In fact, this guy had written more than one paragraph! His words were not only spelled correctly, punctuated and grammatically flawless, but the message also contained nothing sexual at all. It was polite, respectful, courteous and actually quite charming.

He introduced himself and wrote a few lines about who he was and what he was all about, with a brief overview about his likes and dislikes. He mentioned how he equally enjoyed picnics, travel and nature. *Wow, what a delightful surprise!*

I tried not to get too excited, but he was so unique and lovely that I had to respond immediately.

He told me his name was Brandon, a Canadian man living in Brisbane who was looking for new connections. He hardly knew anybody in Australia, and the Internet was his only hope of meeting people. He was ultimately searching for his soulmate but didn't expect to find his on the Internet either. I could certainly understand that.

We began communicating back and forth, and the more we wrote to each other, the more we liked about each other. His words were like magic, filling me with warmth and complete fascination, all underlined with charismatic elocution and a terrific sense of humour. *Could this guy be the one, finally?*

We had so much in common that it seemed we had known each other our entire lives. We swapped photos, chatted for hours online, shared our stories and even some secrets. The more we talked, the more deeply we felt connected. It just felt right to meet, so after a few weeks of chatting, we made arrangements. He offered to drive all the way from the city to meet me and said it would be his pleasure. *Wow.*

The second we met, I was completely blown away. He was drop dead gorgeous for a start, and it only took one hour of having coffee with this guy before I was hooked. He was genuine, respectful, personable, articulate, funny, clearly of high intelligence and most importantly, a perfect gentleman. There was no impropriety whatsoever, and never once did he try to slobber on me or proposition me, nor did he try to lay any claims to me or make the assumption I was now his girlfriend. He didn't even stare down my top!

Being Canadian, he obviously had a completely different upbringing and mindset to the typical Aussie bloke. We continued to sit and talk, completely enthralled in each other, right up until the coffee shop closed. He walked me to my car and saw me off, not even trying to stick his tongue in my mouth or press himself up against me. *What the?*

I drove home absolutely over the moon by how powerful that first meeting was. He was all I could think about for the remainder of the day, all of that night, the entire next day and the rest of that week. Apparently, he felt the same way.

We just *had* to see each other again. We made a date for the following Friday night for dinner, and I almost piddled like an excited puppy when I saw him again. After a charming and eventful few hours of delicious food and enchanting conversation, we went on a moonlight stroll by the beach. When we held hands for the first time, we couldn't let go. Our date was perfect and he was perfect. I had never met anyone so lovely in my entire life.

It took no time at all for my heart to swell with an insurmountable amount of deep and rapturous love for Brandon. I finally discovered what it felt like to completely dissolve in somebody's tight embrace. With just one of his kisses, I would melt. We soon became inseparable and simply couldn't stomach being apart for a minute. It wasn't long before we moved in together. It was like my first real honeymoon, and I was simply ecstatic.

After we settled in and some weeks had passed, Brandon began to notice my odd reactions to certain things. He was quite perplexed by my jumpiness and nerves. It left me with the extraordinarily difficult task of trying to explain, not only to him, but also to myself, and to try to pry open the door that I had clamped shut years ago. My eyes misted up, my voice wavered and at times I became too breathless to continue, but his patience and encouragement allowed me to work my way through it.

Over the weeks and months, mostly during our evening walks, with his prompting, I began to reveal some of the events of my past and the evils that had taken place. I don't know why, but I minimized the effect it had all really had on me, maybe because nobody had cared much before. As he listened, his eyes softened, and his head shook in utter disbelief, followed by a heavy sigh. He didn't have a lot of healing words to offer, but when he reached out and wrapped his arms around me, it felt as if a million angels had carried me gently up into the heavens.

It was the very first hug I had ever received for any ugly

thing that had happened to me. He didn't need to say a word. I felt his love.

I felt sorry that he was getting such a beleaguered woman with so much darkness and shame inside her, but with every story that I purged, I sensed a tremendous release. He reassured me that he was there for me no matter what shadows lurked beneath. For the very first time, I felt that I didn't have to carry the burden alone.

What Brandon had an extremely hard time trying to grasp was the concept of street harassment. He had never personally seen it happening. That was until he came out walking with me.

With his long hair that he would wear in a ponytail, coupled with the darkness of night when we walked, we were often mistaken for two females. That was when he experienced Australian men first-hand. Everything I had been telling him about the streets finally started to sink in. He was beginning to understand what being female in Australia really meant.

The two of us were honked at, whistled at, catcalled, and had men in cars yelling out vile things at us. The first time he heard it, he was absolutely astounded. We had cars slowing down and approaching us too, but when they saw Brandon was actually a male, they would drive away.

"But this isn't right!" he said horrified. "I'm absolutely shocked!"

One evening, he was particularly blown away when an ambulance slowed right down and pulled up beside us. When the young male driver noticed that we weren't two females, he took off in a hurry.

"Even an ambulance driver?!" he questioned, dumbfounded. "Wow that's so unnerving. No wonder you never feel safe!"

On our first Christmas together, we walked around our neighbourhood to look at the twinkly lights and decorated homes, feeling happy and immersing ourselves in the holiday spirit. When we walked out alongside one of the main roads, a car roared by us, and a young male voice yelled out, "Get fucked!"

It shocked Brandon a lot more than it did me. I was used to it. He was floored and couldn't believe how much offensive, hateful behaviour there was in such a beautiful country as ours. He was beginning to understand just how much I had been through.

"I can't believe it. This happens every time we go out!" he said, shaking his head in disbelief.

"Yep!" I shrugged.

He wasn't the first man in my life to have witnessed this behaviour, but he was the first to feel the repugnance of it. He was the first and only one to find it just as deplorable as I did and the only man I'd been with that was just as appalled by it as one should be. He actually cared about the mistreatment of women in our country, and he had never realized how disgusting the behaviour of men could be. He felt ashamed to be associated with other males altogether.

His reactions were hugely comforting to me. It was vindicating to have someone actually agree for the first time that "Hey baby, I'm horny!" was completely unacceptable. He also saw that it happened almost as much during the day, even though I was clearly with him and holding his hand.

"If I went back to Canada and told my friends and family what was going on here, they would have a very hard time believing it," he said. He had been living in Australia for five years and hadn't seen males behave that way before. Being with me opened his eyes to a whole new world, and he very quickly learned that he needed to become more aware of what was happening, not only to Australian women but also to women all over the world.

One evening while we were out celebrating my sister's birthday, I was grabbed on the behind by a bloke who was well into his seventies. I had made the mistake of applauding his terrific dance moves with his lady partner as they left the dance floor. I thought they were great for their age. He walked up, cupped my bottom cheek, gave it a really good squeeze and said, "Thanks darlin', I'll come back for ya!"

Brandon didn't know that had happened until we got home and I told him. He was disillusioned that even older males, who he thought would show some basic manners, had the audacity to do that.

I would often come home after being at work or out shopping with some new story to tell him. It would be some old creep trying to start a dirty conversation with me, someone making some sexual remark, old blokes following me around the supermarket or men chatting me up at work.

"Gee, you can't go anywhere, can you?" he said, astounded.

"Not really, no," I answered.

Over the next few years, I tried to explain that who I was, was the result of a lifetime of this. From the lower end of verbal sexual harassment through to the more serious physical assaults, every encounter had manifested in the same mental and emotional damage. Having been previously victimized by molestation, sexual assault, rape and other acts of violence, sometimes even a simple sexual comment would trigger anything from traumatic flashbacks to panic attacks. It all came out in a variety of ways, and it could take a lifetime for another person to fully comprehend the depths of where it all lay. I didn't expect him to understand fully and still don't.

"I can't do much about what's already happened to you, but I think you would benefit from spending some time away from all this," he said. "I know that street harassment must exist everywhere, especially from what I've been learning lately, but I haven't seen anything to this level of vulgarity in my country, and I am fairly sure you'd be better off in Canada, at least for a while," he added.

"No vulgarity? That sounds like a make-believe world too good to be true!" I said.

"I love you and want you to have some peace in your life. What do you think? Maybe it's worth a try. If I'm wrong, then we can come back, but if I'm right, you will be able to enjoy walking around feeling much safer and a lot more relaxed," he offered, smiling warmly.

If a man was willing to move back to the other side of the world just so I could find some kind of peace and healing in my life, then that was a man who truly loved me.

Sometimes the bravest thing we can do for ourselves is seek peace. It sounded like a marvellous plan.

"Okay, let's do it. What do we have to lose?"

Chapter 28

Preparing for my new life was fairly straightforward. I simply did what needed to be done. Having moved over seventy five times already, starting over was as routine for me as changing my underwear.

It was difficult to imagine a life where all of my fears would be at rest and all of my anxieties melted away. All I had ever known, from my first "backside grab" at twelve years old, was a life of abuse at the hands of men. If a life without that did exist somewhere, whether in Canada or somewhere else, I would embrace it completely and never look back. If not, then I would have lost nothing.

While packing my belongings yet again, I felt that this time was going to be the biggest adventure of them all, at least the most significant. This time, I was finally getting to live out my dreams with someone who my mother referred to as, "The man every woman waits her entire life for."

In the middle of taping up boxes, I couldn't help but wonder where I would be if I hadn't had this life. Would things have turned out any differently? What would I have done, experienced, discovered? Would I have actually had those exciting opportunities that I dreamed of way back when? Would I have travelled more and explored the world as I had planned? Would I have stayed in one place, in one job, or had a fulfilling career? Would I have accomplished something extraordinary? Would I have had loving relationships without anxieties or heartbreak? Would I have been able to trust males and form healthy friendships with them?

I often think about how much of myself I lost to those who stole my dreams. Everything leaves a mark, and all the wishes in the world cannot undo what has taken place, so it is impossible to know where I would have ended up. What I *have* discovered about my journey so far is that I made too many wrong choices, spent too much time in confusion, and let too many rob me of vitally important things.

I still may become the women I was meant to be one day, but it will take time to heal. I need to remind myself that I am more than what I was led to believe. Maybe I actually have something to offer the world, even if it is to share my story.

Maybe there is a young woman reading this who is being sexually harassed in her life right now and struggles to speak up. If she can learn from the mistakes I made and know that she *can* do something about it, then I will feel that I accomplished something meaningful and made a difference to somebody's life.

My story may even resonate with some males, Australian or not, who have never thought about their similar attitudes before. Perhaps by reading this book and realizing how damaging certain behaviours can be, they may want to modify their own.

It would be wonderful for me to at least let those millions of women and girls who suffer at the hands of men every day in every part of the world know that they are not alone. Any woman who is harassed, abused, assaulted or mistreated in any way can know that they *are* important and capable of great things. If anybody can benefit from my story in any way, then it will be worth the colossal effort of having to relive every red-hot, angry moment.

A life of sexual harassment, assault and violation is a life of misery. When women are ripped open by violation early in life, followed by nothing but continual reminders and persistent torment, how are they then expected to try to reach their full potential? Some may turn their noses up at those who have been victims, but it is more difficult to extend a hand of friendship. Those who can, will most likely find the most trusted and loyal friend they've ever had.

Having to say goodbye to my mother was gut wrenching. My father had only recently passed away, his lungs and heart had been failing for a while and he had peacefully passed in the middle of the night two years earlier. He was never far away from Mum, his room being just down the hall from her in their aged care facility where she still lives. She had been mostly confined to her bed and wheelchair for the last few years, but I knew she was in the best place she could be. She has an exceptional level of care and regular visits from the rest of the family. It didn't make it any easier though. It was still going to difficult being that far away from her.

"I can't believe you're actually going!" she said.

"I know. I can hardly believe it myself," I replied, wiping the tears from my cheeks.

"You can always come home, darling."

"That's good to know," I replied, smiling as she rubbed and patted my hand. It always comforted me when she did that.

I took one last look around her room and a final whiff of her scent, taking slow steps towards the door. When I reached it, I blew her a kiss, hoping that one day she would understand why I was leaving.

* * *

As the aircraft levelled out, I smiled softly to myself, knowing that I was leaving all that madness behind. I gently squeezed the hand of my loving partner beside me, and without speaking a word, he understood what it meant. I was thanking him for his support, and for being there with me every step of the way.

For those of you reading my story, I would like to give your hand a squeeze to let you know how grateful I am for keeping me company through every step of my journey.

END

Author Bio

Joy Jennings was born and raised in Melbourne, Australia. At seventeen, she and her family moved to Queensland, where she spent over thirty years living on the Gold Coast.

Following in the footsteps of her father, published author and newspaper columnist, Joy realized her own talents as a writer with the debut of her artfully crafted memoir.

It is Joy's hope that through her work, she can educate young women on how to make the right decisions if experiencing sexual harassment or assault and how to help protect themselves against these actions.

For more information, please visit www.facebook.com/byjoyjennings

Made in the USA
Charleston, SC
25 October 2015